John Merwin's
FLY-TYING
GUIDE

by John Merwin

THE STEPHEN GREENE PRESS
PELHAM BOOKS

THE STEPHEN GREENE PRESS, INC.
Published by the Penguin Group
Viking Penguin Inc., 40 West 23rd Street, New York, New York 10010, U.S.A.
Penguin Books Ltd, 27 Wrights Lane, London W8 5TZ, England
Penguin Books Australia Ltd, Ringwood, Victoria, Australia
Penguin Books Canada Ltd, 2801 John Street, Markham, Ontario, Canada L3R 1B4
Penguin Books (N.Z.) Ltd, 182–190 Wairau Road, Auckland 10, New Zealand

Penguin Books Ltd, Registered Offices: Harmondsworth, Middlesex, England

First published in 1989 by The Stephen Greene Press, Inc.
Published simultaneously in Canada
Distributed by Viking Penguin Inc.

10 9 8 7 6 5 4 3 2 1

CREDITS/ACKNOWLEDGMENTS: Color photographs of fly patterns by William Cheney; all
other photographs by the author. Fly-tying materials in the color plates appear courtesy
of Hunter's Angling Supplies, New Boston, NH 03070. All fly patterns illustrated were
tied by the author, except as follows, which also appear courtesy of Hunter's: Adams,
all Atlantic Salmon Flies, Ausable Wulff, Ballou Special, Bitch Creek, Black/White Hairbug, Black Ghost, Black Nose Dace, Black Woolly Bugger, Crazy Charlie, Cream Variant,
Dark Edson Tiger, Dark Hendrickson, Dun Variant, Elkhair Caddis, Glass Minnow,
Golden Demon, Gray Fox Variant, Gray Ghost, Gray Wulff, Grizzly Wulff, Hendrickson,
Joe's Smelt, Lefty's Deceiver, Letort Cricket, Letort Hopper, Light Cahill, Light Edson
Tiger, March Brown, Martinez, Mickey Finn, Montana, Muddler Minnow, Nine Three,
Prince, Quill Gordon, Quill Gordon (wet), Red Quill, Royal Wulff, Stu Apte Tarpon Fly,
Supervisor, Tan Bonefish Special, Ted's Stonefly, White Marabou Muddler, White Wulff,
Zonker, Zug Bug. The Llama shown on page 35 was tied by Eric Leiser.

Library of Congress Cataloging-in-Publication Data
Merwin, John.
    [Fly-tying guide]
    John Merwin's fly-tying guide / John Merwin.
        p.   cm.
    ISBN 0–8289–0701–3
    1. Fly tying.   I. Title.   II. Title: Fly-tying guide.
SH451.M46 1989   88-23577
688.7'912 — dc19   CIP

Set in Garamond Light by Martha Poole Merwin Graphic Design.
Designed and Produced by Martha Poole Merwin Graphic Design.
Printed in Singapore through Palace Press.

THEY WERE THE WORST LOOKING FLIES I can recall. The proportions were all wrong, and the bodies were marred by lumps and bumps in the tinsel and fur. But if I could get my leader through the hook eye, a task sometimes made difficult as the eyes of my flies were often plugged by errant materials and head cement, the flies sometimes caught trout. I was only 9 or 10 years old at the time, and more than 30 years later the thrill of taking a fish on a fly of my own is undiminished. The flies, I like to think, have improved with practice.

Then, even as now, the start of trout season happened long before opening day in the spring. Brothers, father, uncle, and I gathered around the kitchen table in midwinter, filling out order forms to the mail-order houses whose fur, feathers, hooks, and tinsels would be the fulfillment of our winter dreams. Then, from amid the littered scraps of fly tying, I would hold up and admire a newly minted bucktail, knowing with all certainty that this creation would take the big brown trout I saw under the bridge last season but never caught.

Most fishermen are optimists, and with optimism comes anticipation. Fly tying is a wonderful combination of both, which is part of what makes it such an enjoyable hobby. In this short book, I'll offer enough basic instruction to get you started and a few fly patterns that will work for you no matter where in the country you might fish. Included with each fly pattern is a key to its relative difficulty (1 being easiest, 5 being hardest). If you're new to fly tying, try the easier flies first. I've also indicated with each pattern the kinds of fish most commonly caught with it—everything from trout to tarpon, depending on the fly.

As you become more involved in fly tying, you'll want more detailed references. My old friend Eric Leiser has written three books that cover all aspects of fly tying, and I recommend them to you: *Fly-Tying Materials* (Nick Lyons Books, New York), *The Complete Book of Fly Tying* (Knopf, New York), and *The Book of Fly Patterns* (Knopf, New York). From there, you'll find dozens of other books available at intermediate and advanced levels. There's no substitute for hands-on instruction, so taking lessons is also a good idea. If there's a fly shop in your area, a fly-tying course may be offered in the winter months. At the very least, perhaps you can talk a fly-tying friend into giving you some pointers. Your first attempts may not look like the flies I've illustrated in this book, but don't be discouraged. Even your scruffiest flies will probably take fish, and as you get better, your fishing will likewise improve.

There are dozens of books—both in and out of print—that deal solely with fly tying, a tradition that extends back at least 1,600 years and probably further. This book is a very humble addition to that chain and in many ways a frustrating one as I flip its pages. There simply isn't room here to recount what I've learned through years of fishing and tying sessions with other, more accomplished anglers around the world. I watched quietly from the tail of a pool last night as my 10-year-old son in the riffle above took his first trout on a fly he'd tied himself. We both laughed quite a bit later in the evening— he for his thoughts, I for mine. I hope somewhere in these pages you'll find a path to the sheer joy of that discovery.

John Merwin, Dorset, Vermont   June 1988

KEY TO FISH SPECIES: With each fly pattern presented later in this book, I've included a key to those fishes most commonly caught with that particular fly. Because a particular fish and a fly pattern isn't matched in this book doesn't always mean that the combination is unworkable, just that it's infrequent. I've omitted some fish that are seldom (but should be) sought with flies, such as muskellunge. And, although many of the Atlantic-salmon flies in these pages will work for steelhead and vice versa, I haven't indicated the crossover. Most trout flies are simply listed as being for all trout. Here in alphabetical order are the abbreviations I've used and the fishes they represent:

AS = Atlantic salmon, B = bluefish, BF = bonefish, BkT = brook trout, LLS = landlocked salmon, LMB = largemouth bass, NP = northern pike, P = pickerel, PF = panfish (sunfish, crappies, and perch), PT = permit, SB = striped bass, SD = shad, SMB = smallmouth bass, SS = silver (coho) salmon, SST = southern sea trout, ST = steelhead, TN = tarpon, and WF = northern weakfish.

NO FLY-TYING BOOKS that I can recall have deliberately shown poorly constructed flies as a means of helping you to make better ones. Here are some good and bad ones side by side so you can check points of comparison, a few of which I've highlighted with arrows. Don't feel too bad if some of your early attempts look like those on the right; even those will catch a few fish! Correct techniques for these flies are illustrated in the following pages.

BUCKTAILS:

The tinsel body at right has been roughly wound, showing bumps and gaps. The wing material is too long and too much has been used. The head at right is too long and fat, and the hair butts weren't trimmed at an angle so the head appears lumpy.

WET FLIES:

The quill wings on the fly at right are too full and cocked too high. The tail is too short, and the hackle is too long. The body is too short and not tapered. Too many turns of thread were used to finish the head, making it too large.

NYMPHS:

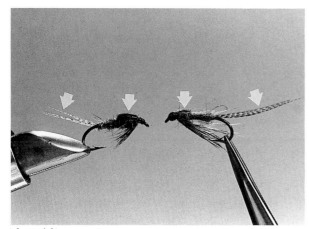

The tail fibers on the nymph at right are too long and not separated. The dubbed body isn't tapered. The wing case and abdomen are too short and slim. The hackle is too long, and the head is too blunt and fat.

DRY FLIES:

The Adams dry fly at right has too short a tail. The body is too short and not tapered. The wings are much too long, as is the hackle. The brown hackle is also much longer than the grizzly: mixed hackle colors should match in length. The head, while of a good size, shows stray hackles bound down over the hook eye.

YOU CAN'T TIE GOOD FLIES without using good tools. It's as simple as that, so as you assemble your equipment remember not to scrimp in this department. Until the 1940s, and for centuries before that time, the only special tool tiers used was a vise to clamp the hook. Many tiers even dispensed with a vise and used their fingers to hold the hook while tying a fly. A few people—Lee Wulff is a notable example—still do this, and it's a handy (but difficult) skill to have in a pinch.

You'll need a vise, a thread bobbin, scissors, a half-hitch tool, a bobbin cleaner/threader, a bodkin, a stacker, and a pair of hackle pliers. For beginners who haven't yet learned all the right fly proportions, I'll add a hackle gauge or similar fly-tier's gauge. A good-quality set of tools may range in price from $70 to more than $300 but will supply years of use for most amateur tiers.

FLY-TYING VISE: Your vise needs to (1) hold your hook securely without damaging it, (2) be adjustable to a convenient working height, and (3) have adjustable jaws to accommodate hooks of various sizes. The Thompson Model "A" vise has been a standard for more than 60 years, but there are many others available. Most, but not all, vises are of a draw-collet design where a lever on one end pulls the jaws back into a tube, forcing them to close and hold the hook. The degree of pressure exerted by the vise jaws depends on how hard you push down on the lever. If it is too loose, the hook will slip. But if you push too hard, the hook will break, either in the vise or (worse) later on when you hook a fish. Put a hook in the vise as shown in the techniques section photographs, and clamp it in place. Tick the hook eye with your fingernail. If the hook makes a dull "dunk" sound, it's too loose. Tighten a little more. Now tick the hook eye again. There should be a sharp "ding" sound if the hook is fastened tightly enough. *Don't apply more pressure beyond this point.*

BOBBIN: Your bobbin will (1) allow you much better control of the tying thread than if you use just your fingers, (2) keep any roughness on your fingertips from abrading the thread, and (3) keep tension on the hanging thread while your hands are busy getting other fly materials. Thread tension on most bobbins is adjustable by bending the two arms that support the thread spool.

SCISSORS: Fly-tying scissors should have (1) fine, well-meshed points for delicate cuts in close quarters and (2) finger loops big enough to fit comfortably. Since deerhair and some synthetic materials dull scissors quickly, you might want to have two pair, using one pair for rough work only.

HACKLE PLIERS: Almost all hackle pliers work by releasing when you squeeze them and grabbing when you release pressure. Yours should hold the tip of a hackle feather firmly without cutting the feather itself. Some commercial products may have a burr or sharpness on a jaw edge, which you can remove with a fine file and sandpaper.

BOBBIN CLEANER/THREADER: Because many fly-tying threads are prewaxed on the spool, you will eventually get a wax buildup in the bobbin tube that interferes with your tying. A bobbin cleaner is a simple rod of a slightly smaller diameter than the bobbin tube. Push it through to remove the wax. At the other end of the same tool is a long spring-wire loop that you can insert through the bobbin tube and use to pull the end of your thread through the tube.

HALF-HITCH TOOL: This provides an easy way to make half-hitch knots on the fly during the tying process. Assuming you're a right-handed tier (lefties, please reverse directions), hold the tool in your right hand and make one turn of thread clockwise around the front of the tool. Slip the tool's opening over the hook eye. Pull left and downward to slide the knot off the tool and onto the fly. Simple. I should point out that most practiced tiers almost never need such a knot as a temporary way of holding things together, since the hanging thread bobbin maintains a controlling tension, but for beginners it's an expedient knot for keeping things under control during the tying process.

BODKIN: This is simply a sharp needle, the dull end of which is inserted into a handle. Buy one or make your own. You'll need it for applying head cement, among other things.

STACKER: This two-part device allows you to easily align hair fibers for wings and tails. Having cut a bunch of hair the right size for your fly, put the hair in the stacker *tips down.* Tap the stacker a few times on a hard surface. Hold the stacker horizontally and slide it apart. The upper half will be holding your material with the tips perfectly aligned and ready for use.

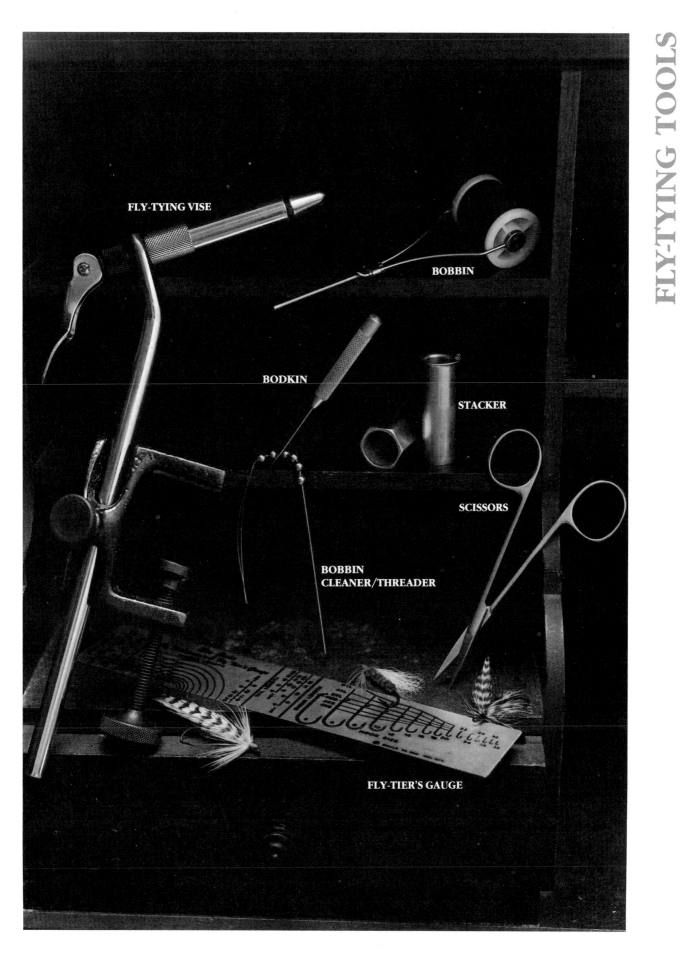

FLY-TYING VISE

BOBBIN

BODKIN

STACKER

SCISSORS

BOBBIN
CLEANER/THREADER

FLY-TIER'S GAUGE

STARTING THE THREAD:

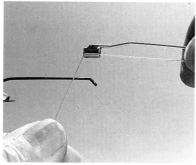

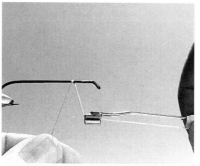

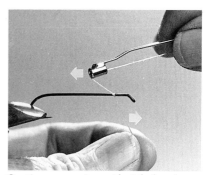

Free end of thread held in left hand, bobbin in right. Hold thread against hook shank at a slight angle as shown.

Make a half-turn around the hook shank as shown while maintaining tension with both hands. Oversize thread has been used here for clarity.

Continue wrapping with right hand at an angle to the rear while moving the left hand to the right, causing the thread to wrap over itself. Trim the loose end after six to eight wraps.

FASTENING MATERIALS:

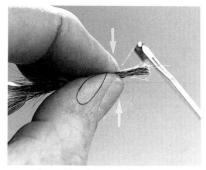

Here's an important way of tying materials to the hook shank. Left thumb and index finger, viewed from above, hold material in position while thread dangles below.

Rock thumb and finger backward. Material is still grasped against the shank, but now you can bring thread up between tips of finger and thumb.

Bring thread back down the other side, then rock finger and thumb forward to trap thread loop above shank. Pull downward with right hand while maintaining left-hand grip. Repeat.

TYING THE WHIP-FINISH KNOT:

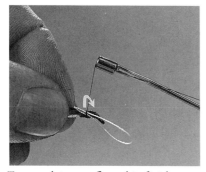

To complete your fly a whip-finish knot is best. Place a loop of thread (at least as strong as your tying thread) against the fly head and make five wraps from left to right.

Push a finger of your right hand against the head to keep things together while you cut the tying thread and put the end through the loop.

Pull the loop with your left hand. This will pull the tying thread to the left and back under the wraps you just made. Trim the tying thread close to the head.

WORKING WITH DEERHAIR:

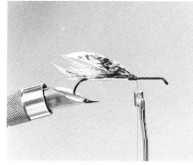

A size 4 Muddler Minnow ready for deerhair head. I've whip-finished the 6/0 thread here and started heavier 3/0 Monocord. Note that forward portion of shank has been left bare.

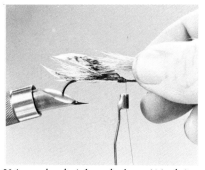

Using a deerhair bunch about ¼ inch in diameter, hold the butts in your right hand and measure the tips for length as hackle against the fly.

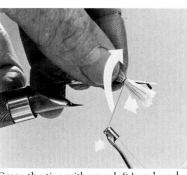

Grasp the tips with your left hand, and then make two loose turns of thread around the butts and hook shank.

Pull on the thread and release your left-hand grip at the same time. As you pull, make two more thread wraps through the now-spinning deerhair.

Use your right thumb and index finger to compress the deerhair toward the rear of the hook. Do this tightly for each succeeding bunch of hair.

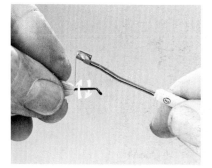

Make two wraps of thread around the shank ahead of the last bunch and compress once again with your right thumb and index finger. Now you're ready for the next bunch of hair.

Once again, make two loose turns over the second bunch, pull and take two additional wraps as you're pulling. Add more bunches of hair as described until you reach the eye of the hook.

Now all hair bunches have been spun on the shank, and you're ready for a whip-finish knot. You may need to use smaller bunches of hair to get close to the hook eye.

I like to sculpt spun hair with a single-edged razor blade to get a finished shape. You can also use scissors to get the head shape shown on page 39.

TYING A BUCKTAIL:

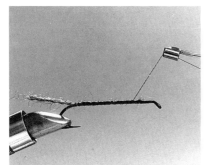

Start thread behind hook eye, and then tie in a strand of red wool yarn somewhat longer than hook shank. Hold yarn in your left hand and wrap over with thread to a point near bend as shown. Bring thread forward again.

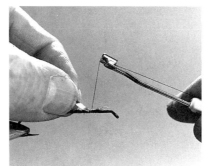

Binding the yarn down over the full body length has given a smooth base for the tinsel. Now tie in Mylar tinsel, silver side up, about ¼ inch behind hook eye with four turns of thread and let bobbin hang in this position.

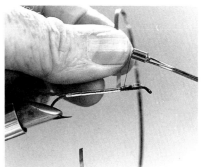

Wrap the tinsel toward the rear of the hook with even turns that butt one another and don't overlap. Stop at the last thread-wraps over the red yarn and come forward. When you reach the hanging thread, unwrap the tinsel end and use your forward wrapping of tinsel to bind down underlayers.

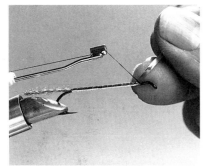

At a point about 3/16 inch behind hook eye, hold tinsel firmly with right hand while making four turns of thread behind tinsel with your left. This binds free end of tinsel, which should then be closely trimmed.

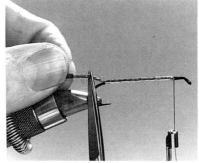

Trim tail to length as shown. You may wish to put a little head cement on the thread wraps where the wing will be tied in to make the fly more secure. This is a good idea after every construction stage of most flies.

Cut a bunch of gray squirrel tail fibers about ⅛ inch in diameter and check for length as shown, holding butts in your right hand. Without moving your right hand, grasp both wing and hook shank with your left thumb and forefinger at the point where the thread is hanging.

Having released your right-hand grip, you're now holding the wing firmly in position with your left hand. Using the finger-and-thumb rocking method described on page 8, bind the wing to the hook shank with 8 to 10 firm thread wraps.

Cut the wing butts at an angle behind the hook eye as shown. This angle cut will give your fly a neat head and also allows the thread to hold all the hair more tightly. Add a drop of cement after trimming and before covering the hair butts with thread.

A small neat head has been completed with wraps of tying thread, and the fly is ready for the whip-finish knot shown on page 8. Several coats of head cement, with drying time between coats, will produce an attractive, glossy finish.

TYING A WET FLY:

This particular wet-fly pattern is a Leadwing Coachman with the addition of a brown hackle tail. Start by tying in narrow gold Mylar tinsel near midshank. Wind the tinsel down toward the hook bend and back to form a tag.

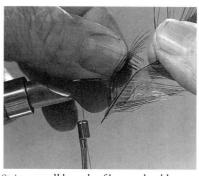

Strip a small bunch of brown hackle fibers from a soft hackle feather, check for length, and tie in butts forward of tinsel tag. We'll be tying them down farther back shortly, and the herl body will cover all the tying in we've done near midshank.

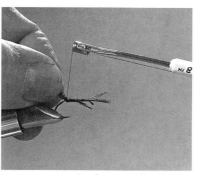

Tie in two strands of peacock herl by their tips where the hackle butts were tied in. Once again, a little planning has been used here that you can use for many flies: if you can, tie in materials where the tie-in bulk will be later hidden, usually under a tapered body.

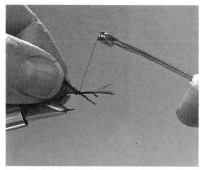

Now hold the herl fibers and the tail fibers together in your left hand and wind thread rearward and over them with your right. Continue back over the tinsel until only two or three tinsel wraps are left showing, which means you'll have a small, neat tinsel tag under the tail fibers.

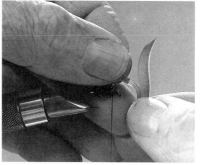

Trim the excess fiber and herl butts, then twist the herls around the tying thread for strength and wind the assembly forward to create a neatly tapered body. Cut sections from matching (left and right) mallard quills. If your section is too large, peel away a few fibers as shown.

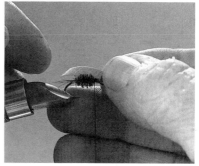

This winging method I learned from Charles Krom, who does it much better than I do. It's easier than more traditional methods, and the lower set of the wings is more effective. Hold the far side wing with the feather curving naturally inward toward the body.

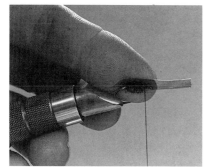

Use pressure with your left index finger to trap the quill wing against the body so the wing covers the upper half only. Then add your left thumb grip on the near side and bind the wing with two thread turns using the "rocking method" on page 8.

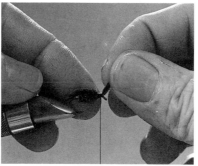

By pulling gently up or down on the wing butt, you can adjust the wing's position before making another two securing thread wraps. Apply the near side wing in similar fashion so the wings curve toward one another and cup the fly's upper body.

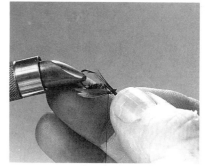

Some tiers wind on hackle before applying the wings, but the following is easier. Simply strip a few soft, brown hackle fibers from a feather, measure for length (to hook point), and tie in under eye. I've inverted the hook in the vise to make this even simpler.

TYING A NYMPH:

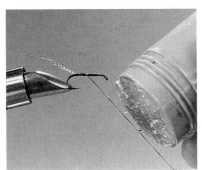

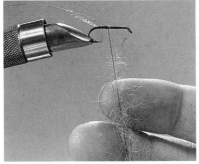

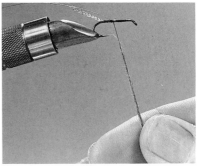

For this fly I've tied in three wood duck flank fibers for tails and have tied in fine oval gold tinsel ribbing at midshank. One turn of thread behind the tails keeps them raised and separated. For a dubbed body, first stroke the tying thread with a tacky dubbing wax as shown.

I've plucked (not cut) the tan underfur from a hare's mask. The loose fur is being held to the thread here by simple adhesion to the wax. Try to use less fur at the ends and more in the middle to eventually achieve a tapered body.

I'm spinning the fur on the thread by rolling the fur and thread between my right thumb and index finger. The rolling motion should be in one direction only and will produce a tight fur "yarn."

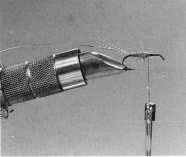

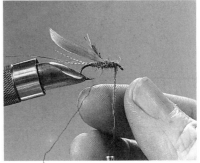

I've wound the thread to the rear while holding the tinsel in my left hand to locate the tinsel at the rear of the body. Then I wound the dubbing forward, increasing in body thickness to just forward of midshank.

I've tied in a section of gray mallard quill slightly wider than the body and am ready to add hackle. I've stroked several fibers back from the tip of a soft, brown partridge hackle and will tie in the stem on top of the duck quill at the point of separation with the hackle tip toward the front of the fly.

I've put more dubbing on the thread and wound the fur thorax. But I have too much dubbing on the thread! No problem—just pluck off the excess. Whatever you do, don't make an ungainly body for the sake of using up extra dubbing.

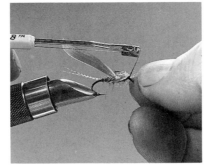

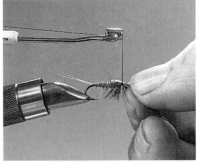

Now I'm winding the tinsel forward over the body in five evenly spaced turns. Use five turns for all your nymphs that require ribbing. If you experiment, you'll find that three or four are too few and six or seven are too many for all but the very largest flies.

Now pull the hackle stem forward with your right hand and tie down with two thread wraps using your left hand. More wraps are unnecessary as the quill wingcase will be pulled forward and bound down in the same spot.

Pull the wingcase forward and hold firmly while tying down with your left hand. Thread compression will pull the wingcase down slightly on each side, forcing the hackle fibers downward in a natural-insect configuration. Complete a neat head and whip-finish.

TYING A DRY FLY:

Form a thread base for the wings, taking care to leave a short section of shank bare behind the hook eye. I'm holding here a section of bronze mallard flank that we'll use for an undivided upright wing. After cutting the section, fold it in half lengthwise twice—a so-called rolled wing.

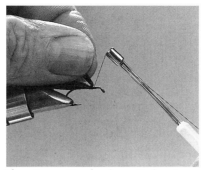

The wing section has been tied on top of the hook shank with the fiber tips forward. Now, while holding the wing, I'm taking a few turns of thread in front to hold the wing upright, taking care to leave some bare hook shank between the wing and hook eye.

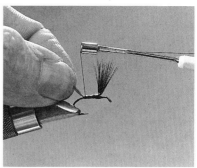

Having trimmed the wing butts neatly at an angle, I've added a bunch of stiff hackle fibers for a tail and am tying them toward the hook bend. You could, at this stage, use figure-eight wraps to divide the wing into two upright sections, but I don't always take the trouble.

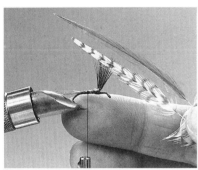

Two dry-fly hackles—one grizzly, one brown—that have been matched for fiber length and partly stripped near the butts for tying in and trimming. Mixing two or three hackles of different colors is a common practice to achieve a more natural effect.

Hackles have been tied in and I've started the dubbed body. I'm winding toward the rear so the bare thread will be used up just as I come to the base of the tail, at which point I'll start winding the dubbed thread forward.

I've wound the brown hackle using two turns behind the wing and three in front, my usual rule of thumb. I'm using only two turns of thread to bind down the hackle tip, which I'll leave untrimmed for the time being.

Now I'm winding the grizzly hackle through the brown. I use a left-and-right rocking motion as I wind, which helps to prevent the brown hackles from being wound down under the grizzly. Once again, I'll use only two thread wraps to bind the grizzly hackle tip and leave it untrimmed.

Here's the reason we left some bare hook shank earlier. Use the fingernails of your right thumb and index finger to compress the wound hackle firmly to the left, toward the wing. Tug on the tying thread to take up any new slack and repeat.

The compression leaves you with both dense hackle and a clear spot for making a small, neat head, ready here for a whip-finish. Dry-fly proportions are usually simple: The hackle tips, hook bend, and tail tips should generally lie in a straight line.

FLY-TYING MATERIALS have always been extraordinarily diverse. The only limiting factor is your imagination—and ultimate acceptance by the fish, of course. Happily, most materials are relatively inexpensive, which means you can accomplish quite a bit right away with a fairly small investment. Most large sporting-goods stores carry a line of packaged materials. If there's a fly shop in your area it may have a broader selection, offering at the same time a chance to pick through bins of material to find exactly what you want. Finally, there are many national mail-order houses that specialize in fly tackle and tying materials, and they can usually supply what you need if time or distance is your problem. These suppliers advertise consistently in fly-fishing and other sporting magazines, where you can find their addresses.

If you are buying by mail and are a little uncertain as to exactly what you want for a particular series of flies, tell the mail-order company in a letter what you plan to do with the material. For example, explaining that you're ordering saddle hackle for saltwater streamers when you send your order in should allow the person who picks and packs your order to send you longer saddle hackles than might be sent for smaller freshwater streamers.

Fly-tying materials are often grouped according to category as follows: *threads,* for tying your fly; *tinsels, flosses,* and *wools,* for fly bodies; *hair,* for tails and wings; *tails,* for tails and wings; *furs,* mostly for dubbed fly bodies; *quills,* tail or wing feathers usually for fly wings and tails; *plumage,* body feathers with a variety of uses; and *hackles,* usually the neck and rump (saddle) feathers of a domestic chicken, for drys, wets, and streamers. Various *cements* and *lacquers* are used at different stages of fly construction, as are some *synthetic materials.* Let's review these categories in more detail.

THREADS: Fly-tying thread should be sufficiently fine to avoid unnecessary bulk in the tying process, yet strong enough to make fly tying practical. It should also be as rot-proof as is practical for the sake of durability. Don't use regular cotton sewing thread for your flies; it rots very quickly.

Until the revolution in synthetic fibers brought about by World War II, silk was the basic choice. Waxed silk thread is strong for its diameter and doesn't stretch. Many traditionalist tiers still prefer silk. Now, however, the standard is prewaxed nylon thread in a 6/0 size and in various colors, which is specified for most of the patterns in this book.

Thread sizes are indicated by a number-and-letter system. Size 1/0 is thicker than size 3/0 (also designated as 000), which is thicker than size 6/0. The finest you might encounter is 9/0 silk, but this is uncommon. Above size 1/0, sizes are designated by letters, with size A being finer than size E, for example. Both the 6/0 nylon and 3/0 Monocord threads specified in this book's patterns are "untwisted," so they wind more flatly on the hook shank than conventional department-store threads.

TINSELS, FLOSSES, WOOLS: Tinsels used to be entirely metal, while body flosses were made of silk. Today, most tinsels are made of Mylar, which is much easier to work around your fly than metal. Most Mylar tinsels are available in various widths and are silver on one side and gold on the other, which makes your fly-tying life quite simple, since the same tinsel can be used for either gold or silver bodies and ribbing. Gold or silver oval tinsels of varying diameters are usually used for ribbing. Flosses are typically multi-stranded, with each strand comprising many very-fine-diameter filaments. They are untwisted, which allows the formation of a smooth, evenly contoured body when wrapped on a hook. Flosses are available in a wide variety of colors and are most commonly made of nylon or rayon. Wool yarn in a variety of colors and sizes is used for the bodies of many wet patterns. Wool is a poor choice for dry-fly bodies as it absorbs water rapidly. Chenille is a fuzzy, yarnlike material consisting of rayon fibers woven into a thread core. It comes in a variety of diameters and many different colors.

HAIR: I use this term to mean pieces of hide with hair attached from the body area (other than the tail) of various mammals that are used for purposes other than body-dubbing fur. Among the samples illustrated on page 18, both black bear and gray fox are used for winging, as the length, color, and texture of the guard hairs make them appropriate for Atlantic salmon and steelhead wet-fly patterns. Others, such as elk, caribou, and deer body hair, have hollow fibers that float well and that can be spun around a hook shank and trimmed to shape. Woodchuck is often used as a wing material for both dry and wet flies, but you'll have to collect your own—supplies are too erratic for it to appear in most shops.

TAILS: The tails of various mammals typically feature longer-fibered hair than bodies and are thus more appropriate for assorted winging applications. Bucktails (deer tails) have the longest hair of any of the commonly sold tails. They are available in a rainbow of dyed colors and are usually used for medium- to very-large-size flies. Calf tails have shorter, finer-textured hair and are usually used for smaller flies. Their fibers tend to be more crinkly than bucktail; try to get the straightest fibers possible. Mink and ermine tails have stiff, glossy fibers, which make them ideal for some dry-fly wings. Squirrel tails (both red and gray species) have long, soft, mottled fibers that move well in the trout stream's currents when used as wet-fly wings. These are also available dyed various colors. For smaller flies, the shorter-fibered pine squirrel tail is ideal. Monga tails are barred black and white and share the soft texture of squirrel.

FURS: Although many of the foregoing animals also offer good dubbing fur under longer guard hairs, the following types of animal body fur are used primarily for dubbed bodies. Beaver body fur is very soft and easily worked as dubbing. It's generally available in both dark natural shades and bleached to a light tan, which I use for my Light Cahills (wet and dry versions) and similar patterns. A hare's mask is just that: the skin and ears of a hare's head, the fur from which is used in such flies as the Gold-ribbed Hare's Ear nymph. Muskrat is very important dubbing fur for such gray-bodied flies as the Muskrat nymph and the Adams dry. Squirrel skins (red or gray species) also offer useful dubbing fur for such flies as the Squirrel Hair nymph.

The most important dubbing fur, however, is rabbit. Domestic rabbits come in a wide variety of natural colors, and most fly-tying suppliers offer rabbit hair in many dyed colors as well. The fur is very soft and easy to blend with other colors and types of fur (use an electric blender) and works very easily and well as dubbing for all types of trout, salmon, and bass flies—large and small.

QUILLS: The term "quill" really has three fly-tying meanings: with reference to a general materials category, it means the primary and secondary wing feathers (and sometimes the large tail feathers) of various birds. It also refers to the center stem of *any* feather. Lastly, quill bodies are often made from the center stem of hackle feathers, peacock herl strands with the fibers removed, or wound with a single fiber from a large primary feather of a turkey or goose. As to materials, primary feathers are the largest flight feathers on a bird wing (secondary feathers are the next largest).

Commonly used quills include those from mallard (for small flies) and goose (for larger flies), both of which are available in a wide range of dyed colors. These are primarily used for wet- and dry-fly wings. Mottled brown-and-gray turkey wing quills are also important for hopper and muddler flies. These have gotten increasingly scarce as more and more farmers now raise white turkeys instead of brown. Brown-and-black-barred turkey tail feathers are also widely used. The short fibers on one side of a large goose quill are referred to as "stripped goose" when stripped from the quill and dyed.

PLUMAGE: The body feathers of various birds may have the greatest variety of uses of any class of fly-tying material. The skin of a male ring-necked pheasant, for example, offers tail feathers for the Pheasant Tail and other nymphs, saddle feathers (also called "church-window" feathers for their color pattern) for stonefly nymphs, and long-fibered rump feathers for such wet flies as the Carey Special. A golden pheasant skin gives the added bonus of golden crest feathers and orange-and-black tippet feathers (from the neck area) used in the Royal Coachman and countless other flies. Flank feathers from the wood duck and mallard are widely used for winging dry and wet flies; these feathers come from the side of the bird's body under the wings, hence the name "flank." Most mallard flank feathers are finely black-and-gray barred, but a few feathers from most birds also have a bronze tint over the barring, hence the name "bronze mallard flank."

Body feathers from guinea fowl are used for a variety of wet flies and, most commonly, for the Muskrat nymph. Neck feathers from the Lady Amherst pheasant are important in some salmon-fly patterns, and the body feathers from an ostrich (small "plume" feathers) have long, soft fibers used in nymph bodies and as a topping for some streamer wings. Breast, neck, and head feathers from the common ruffed grouse or Hungarian partridge make wonderfully soft, mottled hackle for wets and nymphs. Feathers of an African stork called the marabou were once used for many streamers and a few nymphs, but now the term "marabou" is used for the soft, flowing underfeathers from turkeys, which are available in a variety of dyed colors. Peacock herls are long fibers from peacock tail feathers; together with the shorter fibers from peacock "sword" feathers, they are among the most widely used of materials. Finally, but by no means exhausting the choices, silver pheasant body feathers are often used as "shoulders" on streamer patterns.

HACKLE: The term "hackle" usually refers to domestic chicken feathers. Hackle is perhaps the most widely written about and discussed of all fly-tying materials, but the basic concepts here are quite simple. Hackle falls into three categories: wet-fly hackle (usually from a hen); dry-fly hackle (from a rooster); and saddle hackle (also from a rooster), which is used for streamer flies. Hackle is typically sold as the skin from the neck of a hen or rooster, and such skins are generically called "necks."

Feathers from a hen neck are generally broader and softer-fibered than comparable rooster feathers. The softer fibers move well in gentle currents and give a lifelike action to a fly. Hen feathers are "webby." The term "web" in a hackle feather refers to that soft-fibered portion in which the fibers are dull toned and seem to cling together instead of being glossy and distinctly separated from one another. This is typically the lower portion of a given hackle feather, but on hen feathers the web may occupy all or most of the feather itself. Soft, webby hackle is best for wet flies.

Dry-fly necks are from roosters, now often bred for that purpose. Characteristics to look for in your shopping include long, slim feathers relatively free of web. The greater the range of hackle sizes on a neck, the better (and the more expensive). A glossy sheen along the entire surface of the neck is a good indication of relative fiber stiffness.

The highest grade of dry-fly neck (Number 1) may sell for $50, or more in some cases. I use either Number 2 or Number 3 necks for almost all of my own tying, with fine results at a considerable savings. Dry-fly necks are raised both domestically and abroad. Among the best and most widely known commercial necks are those from the Metz Hatchery in Pennsylvania.

Saddle hackle, the long, tapered feathers used for streamers, is sold as a "saddle patch," which is the skin from the rooster's rump where these feathers are found, or as loose or "strung" (sewn-together bundles) hackle. Feather lengths vary widely. Choose very long (seven inches or so) feathers for saltwater and trolling patterns and shorter feathers for smaller freshwater flies. The upper ends of saddle hackle are sometimes used for hackling larger dry flies.

All three hackle types are available in numerous dyed colors, which will be self-explanatory when you encounter them. Brown, black, and white are among the natural colors, but the names of other natural colors can be a little confusing, as they sometimes bear no relation to the actual hackle color. Grizzly hackle is a dark gray (rarely black) feather with white barring. Ginger hackle is a yellowish cream color, while pale ginger may be light cream and dark ginger a yellowish brown. Badger hackle is light tan to creamy yellow, with a dark gray or black center stripe. Furnace hackle is reddish brown with a dark gray or black center stripe. Cree hackle is tricolored, showing bands of light tan, brown, and dark gray or black.

Blue-dun hackle has suffered from description and definition *ad nauseam*. Here's a simple definition: Blue-dun is gray. Color may vary among necks from a very pale gray (almost white) to a dark charcoal gray. Keeping "gray" in mind as you encounter the many descriptions used for shades of blue-dun will save you considerable head scratching.

CEMENTS/LACQUERS: These materials make your fly more durable and occasionally serve a decorative purpose. Common marine spar varnish, straight from the can or thinned, makes a good head cement, especially when used with silk thread. A number of commercial preparations are sold as fly-tying head cement. The important thing is always that the cement be sufficiently thin to flow well into the portion of the fly where it's applied. When you buy head cement, be sure to get the appropriate thinner at the same time.

The so-called super glues are also important, particularly when tying in hair. Applying a drop of super glue to hair butts before covering them with thread will make your fly substantially more durable. Epoxy is commonly used on saltwater flies and for gluing plastic doll eyes to fly heads; the "five-minute" variety is adequate for most uses. Lacquers are used for painting eyes on fly heads. Use lacquers made especially for that purpose, or buy little bottles of model paint at your local store.

Fly-tying wax is critical, especially for making dubbed bodies. Important for holding spun fur on thread, wax used to be the subject of numerous published formulas that bordered on alchemy.

Fly-tying feathers, clockwise from upper left next to reel: wood duck flank (plain and white tipped), black-and-white barred mallard flank, pair of mallard wings, white-spotted guinea fowl, brown partridge, blue- and red-dyed goose quills, mottled turkey quill (under guinea feathers), gray ostrich plume, brown-mottled ring-necked pheasant tail feathers, peacock sword feather, eyed peacock tail feather, black-and-white Lady Amherst pheasant neck, ring-necked pheasant skin, and golden pheasant skin (with yellow crest and orange tippet feathers) at lower left.

Coloration in premium dry-fly necks, clockwise from reel at bottom: brown, silver badger (black striped), medium ginger, grizzly (black-and-white barred), and cree. The three center necks are blue-dun—light, medium, and dark from left to right.

About ten years ago Glenn Overton, now of Libby, Montana, started formulating and marketing his Wonder Wax in an easy-to-use tube, and today this and other brands are widely sold.

SYNTHETIC MATERIALS: Although I've alluded already to a few synthetic materials (nylon and rayon, for example), I'll list here a few of the more important ones used in this book's patterns. Polypropylene is available as a very-fine-fibered dubbing material and as a yarn sometimes used for dry-fly wings. Spectrum, made by the Andra Company, is a very soft synthetic dubbing in many, many dyed colors that I use for almost all my own small dry flies. Fly-Rite is another widely distributed brand. The Ultra-Translucent Nymph Blends, developed by Ken Ligas, are a coarser-fibered synthetic in 50 different dyed and blended colors, suitable for larger dubbed bodies of all types. Listing synthetics is difficult, as many of the smaller companies have gone in and out of business within a short span. Each of the foregoing has been around for at least eight years.

Fishair is a synthetic substitute for bucktail available in lengths of up to 10 inches and in many colors. It's very tough and is often used for saltwater flies. Flashabou is sold as bundled filaments in various metallic colors and adds considerable sparkle when a few strands are tied into a streamer. Krystal Flash is similar to Flashabou, and its kinked surface is even flashier.

Fly-tying furs and tails, clockwise from upper left: gray fox fur, brown-and-white calf tail, black-and-white-barred monga tail, hare's mask, white-tipped gray squirrel tail next to fox (reddish) squirrel tail with a shorter, fibered pine squirrel tail on top, dark (natural) and bleached beaver fur sections, and a natural (brown and white) bucktail. Bottom row, left to right: squirrel skin, natural (dark brown) mink tail, gray-and-brown muskrat fur, elk body hair, caribou body hair, deer body hair, with black bear fur at lower right.

ADAMS
HOOK: Mustad 94840, sizes 10-18.
THREAD: Black nylon, 6/0.
TAIL: Brown and grizzly fibers mixed.
BODY: Gray muskrat dubbing.
WING: Grizzly hackle tips.
HACKLE: Brown and grizzly mixed.
NOTE: An old Michigan pattern, now the country's most popular dry fly.
DIFFICULTY: 4.   SPECIES: All trout, LLS, SMB, PF.

AUSABLE WULFF
HOOK: Mustad 94840, sizes 10-18.
THREAD: Red nylon, 6/0.
TAIL: Woodchuck guard-hair fibers.
BODY: Tan dubbing, or tan blended with small amount of orange.
WING: White calftail, upright and divided.
HACKLE: Brown and grizzly mixed.
NOTE: Hair-wing dry flies are more durable and better floaters than more delicate feather-wings and are better suited to rough pocket-water conditions such as those on New York's Ausable River, where this pattern originated.
DIFFICULTY: 4.   SPECIES: All trout, LLS, AS, ST, SMB, PF.

BLACK FUR ANT
HOOK: Mustad 94840, sizes 10-18.
THREAD: Black nylon, 6/0.
TAIL: None.
BODY: Black dubbing; one ball of fur at rear of hook and a second at the front, leaving room for hackle between the two.
HACKLE: Black.
NOTE: Don't use too much hackle; one or two turns is plenty. This pattern and the Cinnamon Fur Ant are very effective in smaller sizes, use a Mustad 94859 hook, sizes 20-26.
DIFFICULTY: 1.   SPECIES: All trout, LLS, SMB, PF.

BLACK GNAT
HOOK: Mustad 94840, sizes 10-18.
THREAD: Black nylon, 6/0.
TAIL: Black hackle fibers.
BODY: Black dubbing.
WING: Gray mallard quill sections.
HACKLE: Black.
NOTE: One of our oldest recorded fly patterns, versions of which extend back to A.D. 1450.
DIFFICULTY: 4.   SPECIES: All trout, SMB, PF.

BLACK BIVISIBLE
HOOK: Mustad 94840, sizes 10-18.
THREAD: Black nylon, 6/0.
TAIL: Black hackle fibers.
BODY: None.
WING: None.
HACKLE: Black, palmered (wound) forward over hook shank, with a few turns of white at the head.
NOTE: Developed by the late Edward Hewitt. Try experimenting with brown and ginger, also with white in front. Hackle fibers should be progressively longer toward the head of the fly.
DIFFICULTY: 1.   SPECIES: All trout, LLS, SMB, PF.

BLOND HAYSTACK
HOOK: Mustad 94840, sizes 10-18.
THREAD: Cream nylon, 6/0.
TAIL: Cream calftail fibers.
BODY: Cream or ginger dubbing.
WING: Light tan or ginger deerhair, tied upright 1/3 of shank length behind head. Spread deerhair so it fans 180 degrees around the top and sides of shank. Finish with dubbing between wing and head, which helps to hold the wing shape.
HACKLE: None.
NOTE: An excellent and imitative fast-water dry fly developed by Fran Betters along New York's Ausable, this fly was the basis for the later and more publicized Comparadun dry-fly series. Try dark brown for the same pattern.
DIFFICULTY: 2.   SPECIES: All trout, LLS, SMB, PF.

BLUE-WINGED OLIVE
HOOK: Mustad 94840, sizes 10-18.
THREAD: Olive nylon, 6/0.
TAIL: Medium blue-dun hackle fibers.
BODY: Medium olive dubbing.
WING: Two medium blue-dun hackle tips or gray mallard quill sections.
HACKLE: Medium blue-dun.
NOTE: The body color on many kinds of olive-bodied mayflies changes from darker to lighter olive not long after hatching, so you might vary your body colors from very dark to very bright olive in a variety of sizes.
DIFFICULTY: 3.   SPECIES: All trout, LLS, SMB, PF.

BLUE-DUN SPIDER
HOOK: Mustad 94840, sizes 14-16.
THREAD: Gray nylon, 6/0.
TAIL: Blue-dun hackle fibers, 1½ to 2 times normal length.
BODY: Fine flat gold tinsel, short.
HACKLE: Blue-dun, 1½ to 2 sizes larger than normally required for the hook size you're using. A size 14 hook, for example, takes hackle normally used for a size 10.
NOTE: Other good hackle/tail colors are ginger or badger. Often tied on a shorter-than-normal hook (Mustad 94838, for example), but you can also use the standard 94840 dry-fly model specified above.
DIFFICULTY: 2.   SPECIES: All trout, LLS, AS.

CREAM VARIANT
HOOK: Mustad 94840, sizes 10-18.
THREAD: Yellow nylon, 6/0.
TAIL: Cream hackle fibers, slightly longer than normal.
BODY: Cream hackle stem from which fibers have been stripped.
HACKLE: Cream, a size larger than normal for hook size.
WINGS: None.
NOTE: Thoroughly soak hackle stem in water before winding body, to prevent splitting.
DIFFICULTY: 1.   SPECIES: All trout, LLS, SMB.

DUN VARIANT
HOOK: Mustad 94840, sizes 10-18.
THREAD: Olive nylon, 6/0.
TAIL: Medium blue-dun hackle fibers, 1½ times normal length for hook size.
BODY: Rusty brown hackle stem from which fibers have been stripped.
HACKLE: Medium blue-dun, 1½ times normal size.
WINGS: None.
NOTE: The late Art Flick's pattern and a favorite of mine. Soak quill before winding to prevent splitting.
DIFFICULTY: 1.   SPECIES: All trout, LLS, SMB.

ADAMS

BLOND HAYSTACK

AUSABLE WULFF

BLUE-WINGED OLIVE

BLUE-DUN SPIDER

BLACK FUR ANT

BLACK GNAT

CREAM VARIANT

BLACK BIVISIBLE

DUN VARIANT

(Flies shown 2.2 times actual size.)

ELKHAIR CADDIS

HOOK: Mustad 94840, sizes 10-18.
THREAD: Cream nylon, 6/0.
TAIL: None.
BODY: Tan or brown hare's ear dubbing.
RIBBING: Brown hackle palmered over body. This hackle should be a size smaller than normal for the hook you're using.
WING: Tan elkhair or deerhair, tied down and extending very slightly past hook bend.
NOTE: Originated by Al Troth of Montana, this fly has become the prototype for dozens of different caddis patterns. Try various color combinations.
DIFFICULTY: 2.   SPECIES: All trout, LLS, SMB, PF.

GRAY FOX VARIANT

HOOK: Mustad 94840, sizes 10-18.
THREAD: Brown nylon, 6/0.
TAIL: Ginger hackle fibers.
BODY: Medium-ginger hackle stem, stripped.
WING: None.
HACKLE: Grizzly and ginger mixed.
NOTE: A version of Art Flick's adaptation of a pattern by the late Preston Jennings. That sounds a little like "The House That Jack Built," but so goes much of fly tying. Jennings was the first modern American writer to correlate fly patterns and insect hatches, in his *A Book of Trout Flies* (1935).
DIFFICULTY: 2.   SPECIES: All trout, LLS, SMB, PF.

GREEN DRAKE (Eastern)

HOOK: Mustad 94840, sizes 8-12.
THREAD: Olive nylon, 6/0.
TAIL: Ginger hackle fibers.
BODY: Blend of pale yellow and beige dubbing.
HACKLE: Light dun, grizzly, and ginger mixed.
WINGS: Wood duck flank, upright and divided.
NOTE: The so-called Green Drake isn't really green at all, although the adults appear pale yellow-green in flight. One clue to finding this hatch is finding the right sort of stream bottom, as the nymphs are burrowers and require a firm, silty substrate.
DIFFICULTY: 3.   SPECIES: All trout, LLS, SMB.

GREEN DRAKE (Western)

HOOK: Mustad 94840, sizes 8-12.
THREAD: Olive nylon, 6/0.
TAIL: Dark dun hackle fibers.
BODY: Olive green dubbing.
WING: Dark gray mallard quill sections, tied upright.
HACKLE: Dark dun and yellow mixed.
NOTE: Shades of green and yellow and prominent dark wings are keys in imitating the Western Green Drake *(Ephemerella grandis),* a very different fly from the Eastern Green Drake *(Ephemera guttulata)* described previously.
DIFFICULTY: 3.   SPECIES: All trout.

GRIZZLY WULFF

HOOK: Mustad 94840, sizes 10-16.
THREAD: Gray nylon, 6/0.
TAIL: Brown calftail or bucktail fibers.
BODY: Yellow floss.
WING: Brown calftail or bucktail fibers, upright and divided.
HACKLE: Brown and grizzly mixed.
NOTE: When selecting calftail for dry-fly wings and tails, use the straightest fibers available. Calftails often have kinked or twisted hair fibers, which makes straight bucktail a better choice.
DIFFICULTY: 3.   SPECIES: All trout, LLS, AS, ST, SMB, PF.

HENDRICKSON

HOOK: Mustad 94840, sizes 10-18.
THREAD: Brown nylon, 6/0.
TAIL: Dun hackle fibers.
BODY: Urine-stained fox belly fur (dubbing).
WING: Wood duck flank fibers.
HACKLE: Blue-dun.
NOTE: The body material mentioned is traditional: light tan with a pinkish cast. It's also a little esoteric. Just using light tan dubbing will work fine.
DIFFICULTY: 3.   SPECIES: All trout, LLS, SMB.

HENRYVILLE SPECIAL

HOOK: Mustad 94840, sizes 10-18.
THREAD: Olive nylon, 6/0.
TAIL: None.
BODY: Olive floss.
RIBBING: Undersize grizzly hackle palmered forward over body.
WING: Gray mallard wing quill sections tied down along sides.
HACKLE: Brown.
NOTE: Preceding is traditional pattern. You might try orange or bright green bodies and mixing brown and grizzly hackle at the head of this famous adult caddis imitation.
DIFFICULTY: 4.   SPECIES: All trout, LLS, SMB.

LIGHT CAHILL

HOOK: Mustad 94840, sizes 10-18.
THREAD: Cream nylon, 6/0.
TAIL: Pale ginger hackle fibers.
BODY: Cream dubbing fur.
WING: Wood duck flank fibers.
HACKLE: Pale ginger.
NOTE: America's second most popular trout fly, after the Adams.
DIFFICULTY: 3.   SPECIES: All trout, LLS, SMB.

LETORT CRICKET

HOOK: Mustad 94840, sizes 10-18.
THREAD: Black nylon, 6/0.
TAIL: None.
BODY: Black dubbing.
WING: Black-dyed duck or goose wing quill section tied down along top of body.
HACKLE: Black-dyed deerhair, spun at head and trimmed to shape. Leave a few long fibers extending back along side and body.
NOTE: Imitations of hoppers, crickets, ants, etc., are generically called terrestrials and are typically most effective from summer through early fall, when the naturals are active along streams and lakeshores.
DIFFICULTY: 3.   SPECIES: All trout, SMB, PF.

LETORT HOPPER

HOOK: Mustad 94840, sizes 10-18.
THREAD: Yellow nylon, 6/0.
TAIL: None.
BODY: Yellow dubbing.
WING: Brown mottled turkey quill section tied flat over body.
HACKLE: Natural tan deerhair spun at head. Trim to head shape. Leave a few untrimmed fibers extending rearward on top and sides.
NOTE: A simple and effective grasshopper pattern developed almost 30 years ago by Charles Fox and Ernest Schwiebert along Pennsylvania's Letort Spring Run.
DIFFICULTY: 3.   SPECIES: All trout, SMB, PF.

ELKHAIR CADDIS

HENDRICKSON

GRAY FOX VARIANT

HENRYVILLE SPECIAL

GREEN DRAKE (Eastern)

LIGHT CAHILL

GREEN DRAKE (Western)

LETORT CRICKET

GRIZZLY WULFF

LETORT HOPPER

(Flies shown 2.2 times actual size.)

MARCH BROWN

HOOK: Mustad 94840, sizes 10-18.
THREAD: Orange nylon, 6/0.
TAIL: Dark ginger hackle fibers.
BODY: Tan fox fur dubbing.
WING: Wood duck flank feather fibers.
HACKLE: Dark ginger and grizzly mixed.
NOTE: Older versions of this classic by the late Preston Jennings call for a brown-thread ribbing, which is a more realistic imitation.
DIFFICULTY: 3.   SPECIES: All trout, LLS, SMB.

MOSQUITO

HOOK: Mustad 94840, sizes 12-18.
THREAD: Gray nylon, 6/0.
TAIL: Grizzly hackle fibers.
BODY: Two strands moose mane fiber—one dark, one light—wound together to form segmented body.
WING: Grizzly hackle tips.
HACKLE: Grizzly.
NOTE: An easier way to make the body for this fly is by using a stripped grizzly hackle stem, although the dark-and-light segmented effect won't be as pronounced.
DIFFICULTY: 3.   SPECIES: All trout, LLS, SMB.

PALE EVENING DUN

HOOK: Mustad 94840, sizes 14-18.
THREAD: Cream nylon, 6/0.
TAIL: Pale blue-dun hackle fibers.
BODY: Light yellow dubbing fur.
WING: Medium blue-dun hackle tips.
HACKLE: Pale blue-dun hackle fibers.
NOTE: One of many imitations for an early-summer group of mayflies collectively called "sulphurs." For a better imitation, mix a little bright orange dubbing with the yellow at the forward part of the body.
DIFFICULTY: 3.   SPECIES: All trout, LLS, SMB.

QUILL GORDON

HOOK: Mustad 94840, sizes 12-18.
THREAD: Black nylon, 6/0.
TAIL: Blue-dun hackle fibers.
BODY: Stripped peacock quill.
WING: Wood duck flank feather fibers.
HACKLE: Blue-dun.
NOTE: Peacock quill bodies are made by stripping the short, metallic-colored fibers from the herl strip taken from the "eyed" portion of a peacock tail feather. Put the herl strip on a hard, flat surface and use a pencil eraser.
DIFFICULTY: 3.   SPECIES: All trout, LLS, SMB.

RED QUILL

HOOK: Mustad 94840, sizes 10-18.
THREAD: Brown nylon, 6/0.
TAIL: Blue-dun hackle fibers.
BODY: Stripped reddish brown hackle stem. Soak before winding.
WING: Wood duck flank feather fibers.
HACKLE: Blue-dun.
NOTE: Another pattern from the late Art Flick, as described in his book *New Streamside Guide to Naturals and Their Imitations* (Nick Lyons Books, New York). Must reading!
DIFFICULTY: 3.   SPECIES: All trout, LLS, SMB.

ROYAL WULFF

HOOK: Mustad 94840, sizes 10-18.
THREAD: Black nylon, 6/0.
TAIL: Brown calftail or bucktail fibers.
BODY: Peacock herl divided in the middle by a band of red floss.
WING: White calftail or bucktail fibers, tied upright and divided.
HACKLE: Brown.
NOTE: An excellent and durable attractor pattern that has replaced the fragile Fan-wing Royal Coachman of bygone days. This best-known of the Wulff Series now serves as a registered trademark for Joan and Lee Wulff.
DIFFICULTY: 3.   SPECIES: All trout, LLS, AS, ST, SMB, PF.

WHITE WULFF

HOOK: Mustad 94840, sizes 10-18.
THREAD: Cream nylon, 6/0.
TAIL: White calftail or bucktail fibers.
BODY: White dubbing or wool yarn.
WING: White calftail or bucktail, upright and divided.
HACKLE: Badger.
NOTE: This pattern is widely used for both trout and, in larger sizes, Atlantic salmon. It's also a fair imitation of the coffin fly, the spent-spinner stage of the Eastern green drake mayfly.
DIFFICULTY: 3.   SPECIES: All trout, LLS, AS, ST, SMB, PF.

GRAY WULFF

HOOK: Mustad 94840, sizes 10-18.
THREAD: Gray nylon, 6/0.
TAIL: Brown calftail or bucktail fibers.
BODY: Gray dubbing or wool yarn.
WING: Brown calftail or bucktail, upright and divided.
HACKLE: Medium blue-dun.
NOTE: This pattern was the first among the Wulff series developed by Lee Wulff, having been created along New York's Ausable River and Esopus Creek in 1929-30. With this pattern and subsequent others, Wulff popularized the use of animal hair as a dry-fly winging material.
DIFFICULTY: 3.   SPECIES: All trout, LLS, AS, ST, SMB, PF.

RUSTY SPINNER

HOOK: Mustad 94840, sizes 12-18.
THREAD: Brown nylon, 6/0.
TAIL: Light blue-dun hackle fibers, tied long.
BODY: Rust-colored dubbing fur.
WING: Pale gray polypropylene yarn fibers, tied "spent," which means resembling airplane wings.
HACKLE: None.
NOTE: The most common error in making this spent mayfly imitation is using too much winging material. Effectiveness here depends on sparse tying. Pale gray winging material is a much better imitation than the commonly used stark white.
DIFFICULTY: 2.   SPECIES: All trout, LLS, SMB.

WOODCHUCK CADDIS

HOOK: Mustad 94840, sizes 10-18.
THREAD: Brown nylon, 6/0.
TAIL: None.
BODY: Burnt orange dubbing.
WING: Woodchuck guard hairs, tied down and extending slightly beyond hook bend.
HACKLE: Brown and grizzly mixed.
NOTE: Excellent rough-water caddis imitation developed by Eric Leiser. Vary body colors (try olive or gray) with thread color to match.
DIFFICULTY: 3.   SPECIES: All trout, LLS, SMB, PF.

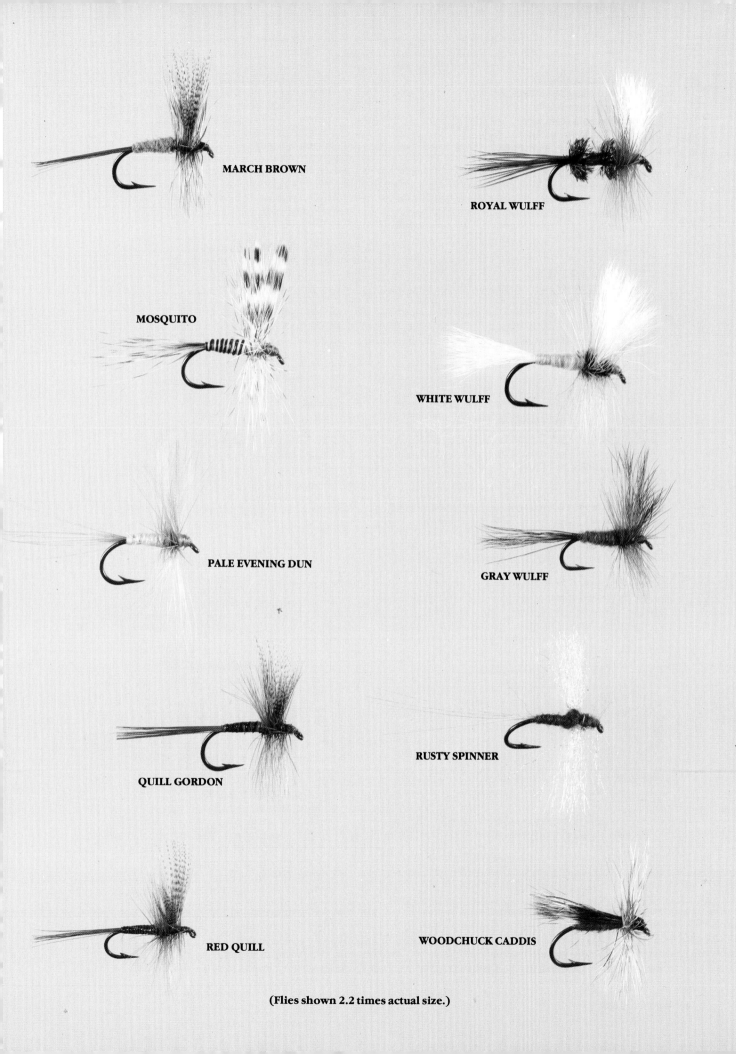

MARCH BROWN

ROYAL WULFF

MOSQUITO

WHITE WULFF

PALE EVENING DUN

GRAY WULFF

QUILL GORDON

RUSTY SPINNER

RED QUILL

WOODCHUCK CADDIS

(Flies shown 2.2 times actual size.)

BLACK GNAT
HOOK: Mustad 3906, sizes 10-16.
THREAD: Black nylon, 6/0.
TAIL: Black hackle fibers.
BODY: Black dubbing fur.
WING: Gray duck quill sections.
HACKLE: Black.
NOTE: In general, slim and graceful wet-fly dressings are more effective than the bulbous and chunky dressings common among the inexpensive commercial flies that clutter hardware-store counters across the country.
DIFFICULTY: 3.   SPECIES: All trout, LLS, SMB, PF.

BREADCRUST
HOOK: Mustad 3906, sizes 10-16.
THREAD: Brown nylon, 6/0.
TAIL: None.
BODY: Orange floss or dubbing fur.
RIBBING: Stripped stem from a reddish brown hackle.
HACKLE: Grizzly.
WING: None.
NOTE: Many wet-fly tiers prefer the slightly longer 3906B hook to the conventional 3906 wet-fly hook specified for these patterns.
DIFFICULTY: 1.   SPECIES: All trout, LLS, SMB, PF.

CAREY SPECIAL
HOOK: Mustad 9672, sizes 6-10.
THREAD: Olive nylon, 6/0.
TAIL: Olive-dyed ring-necked pheasant rump feather fibers.
BODY: Olive chenille or dubbing fur.
RIBBING: Fine gold tinsel.
HACKLE: Olive-dyed ring-necked pheasant rump feather, long.
WING: None.
NOTE: Tied in various color combinations. A Northwestern trout pattern especially effective as a lake fly.
DIFFICULTY: 1.   SPECIES: All trout, LLS, SMB, PF.

LEADWING COACHMAN
HOOK: Mustad 3906, sizes 10-16.
THREAD: Black nylon, 6/0.
TAIL: None.
TAG: Fine flat gold tinsel.
BODY: Peacock herl.
HACKLE: Brown.
WING: Gray mallard quill sections.
DIFFICULTY: 3.   SPECIES: All trout, LLS, SMB, PF.

GOLD-RIBBED HARE'S EAR
HOOK: Mustad 3906, sizes 10-16.
THREAD: Brown nylon, 6/0.
TAIL: Wood duck flank feather fibers.
BODY: Hare's-mask dubbing fur.
RIBBING: Fine oval gold tinsel.
HACKLE: Dubbing fur tufted out from body near head.
WING: Gray duck quill sections.
NOTE: America's most popular wet fly. I like to add partridge hackle to mine, although traditional versions don't call for it.
DIFFICULTY: 3.   SPECIES: All trout, LLS, SMB, PF.

BLUE-WINGED OLIVE
HOOK: Mustad 3906, sizes 10-16.
THREAD: Olive nylon, 6/0.
TAIL: Blue-dun (gray) hackle fibers.
BODY: Medium-olive dubbing fur.
HACKLE: Medium blue-dun (gray).
WING: Gray mallard quill sections.
NOTE: Many *Baetis* mayflies, imitated by this pattern, dive under water as adults to lay their eggs, which helps to account for the effectiveness of this dressing.
DIFFICULTY: 3.   SPECIES: All trout, LLS, SMB, PF.

BROWN HACKLE
HOOK: Mustad 3906, sizes 10-16.
THREAD: Brown nylon, 6/0.
TAIL: Red wool, short.
BODY: Peacock herl.
HACKLE: Brown.
WING: None.
NOTE: Most wet-fly patterns, including this one, are more effective in smaller sizes. As your fly-tying skill increases, try dressing your wet flies in sizes 16 and 18, unless the need to imitate a specific insect calls for a larger size.
DIFFICULTY: 1.   SPECIES: All trout, PF.

GRAY HACKLE YELLOW
HOOK: Mustad 3906, sizes 10-16.
THREAD: Yellow nylon, 6/0.
TAIL: None.
BODY: Yellow floss.
RIBBING: Fine oval gold tinsel.
HACKLE: Grizzly.
WING: None.
NOTE: This pattern—among many others—is also a good lake and pond fly. In one of his old *Field & Stream* columns, A. J. McClane described dressing this pattern with dry-fly oil, fishing it in pulls under the surface, and allowing it to bob to the top between pulls; a technique that's since paid off for me.
DIFFICULTY: 1.   SPECIES: All trout, LLS, SMB, PF.

DARK HENDRICKSON
HOOK: Mustad 3906, sizes 10-16.
THREAD: Brown nylon, 6/0.
TAIL: Wood duck flank feather fibers.
BODY: Gray muskrat dubbing fur.
HACKLE: Medium blue-dun (gray).
WING: Wood duck flank feather fibers.
DIFFICULTY: 2.   SPECIES: All trout, LLS, SMB, PF.

GRIZZLY KING
HOOK: Mustad 3906, sizes 10-16.
THREAD: Black nylon, 6/0.
TAIL: Section of red-dyed duck or goose quill.
BODY: Medium-green floss.
RIBBING: Fine flat silver tinsel.
HACKLE: Grizzly.
WING: Mallard flank feather fibers.
NOTE: Like many of the gaudy Victorian wet-fly patterns that have fallen from favor with anglers in recent times, this green-and-gray pattern does have an entomological basis. It's fairly representative of an egg-laying *Brachycentrus* caddisfly.
DIFFICULTY: 3.   SPECIES: All trout, LLS, SMB, PF.

BLACK GNAT

BLUE-WINGED OLIVE

BREADCRUST

BROWN HACKLE

GRAY HACKLE YELLOW

CAREY SPECIAL

LEADWING COACHMAN

DARK HENDRICKSON

GOLD-RIBBED HARE'S EAR

GRIZZLY KING

(Flies shown 2.0 times actual size.)

LITTLE MARRYAT

HOOK: Mustad 3906, sizes 10-16.
THREAD: Cream nylon, 6/0.
TAIL: Palest ginger hackle fibers, tied long.
BODY: Pale cream-yellow dubbing fur.
HACKLE: Palest ginger.
WING: Pale gray mallard quill sections tied short.
NOTE: George Selwyn Marryat was a 19th-century Englishman who, although he never published a book, was a major influence in the development of modern fly patterns through his work with Halford and others.
DIFFICULTY: 3.   SPECIES: All trout, LLS, SMB, PF.

MARCH BROWN

HOOK: Mustad 3906, sizes 10-16.
THREAD: Brown nylon, 6/0.
TAIL: Wood duck flank feather fibers.
BODY: Hare's-mask dubbing fur.
RIBBING: Fine oval gold tinsel.
HACKLE: Partridge.
WING: Mottled turkey quill sections.
DIFFICULTY: 3.   SPECIES: All trout, LLS, SMB, PF.

PICKET PIN

HOOK: Mustad 9672, sizes 8-12.
THREAD: Black nylon, 6/0.
TAIL: Brown hackle fibers.
BODY: Peacock herl.
RIBBING: Brown hackle.
WING: Gray squirrel tail fibers.
HEAD: Peacock herl wound full.
NOTE: This pattern generally resembles a number of medium-size, dark stoneflies that appear on eastern and midwestern rivers in early spring before and during the major mayfly and caddis hatches. So, in addition to fishing in conventional wet-fly fashion, try fishing this pattern "damp"—lightly dressed and low floating on the surface.
DIFFICULTY: 2.   SPECIES: All trout, LLS, SMB, PF.

ROYAL COACHMAN

HOOK: Mustad 3906, sizes 10-16.
THREAD: Black nylon, 6/0.
TAIL: Golden pheasant tippet fibers.
BODY: Peacock herl and red floss, in thirds as shown.
HACKLE: Brown.
WING: White duck quill sections.
NOTE: In this era of drab, imitative fly patterns, the Royal Coachman is still an effective—albeit gaudy—classic, especially for brook trout.
DIFFICULTY: 3.   SPECIES: All trout, PF.

TELLICO

HOOK: Mustad 3906, sizes 10-16.
THREAD: Brown nylon, 6/0.
TAIL: Guinea hackle fibers.
SHELL: Four pheasant tail fibers tied in at tail and pulled forward over body.
BODY: Yellow floss.
RIBBING: Peacock herl.
HACKLE: Brown.
DIFFICULTY: 2.   SPECIES: All trout, SMB, PF.

LIGHT CAHILL

HOOK: Mustad 3906, sizes 6-16.
THREAD: Cream nylon, 6/0.
TAIL: Wood duck flank feather fibers.
BODY: Cream dubbing fur.
HACKLE: Light ginger.
WING: Wood duck flank feather fibers.
NOTE: In larger sizes, meaning as large as size 6 or 8, this is an effective fly when night fishing for brown trout.
DIFFICULTY: 2.   SPECIES: All trout, LLS, SMB, PF.

PARTRIDGE AND ORANGE

HOOK: Mustad 3906, sizes 10-16.
THREAD: Brown nylon, 6/0.
TAIL: None.
BODY: Orange floss.
HACKLE: Partridge, long.
WING: None.
NOTE: A venerable Western European pattern and part of a series known as "partridge and...," consisting of partridge hackle and variously colored floss bodies.
DIFFICULTY: 1.   SPECIES: All trout, LLS, PF.

TAN CADDIS PUPA

HOOK: Mustad 3906, sizes 10-16.
THREAD: Tan nylon, 6/0.
TAIL: None.
BODY: Tan dubbing fur.
HACKLE: Brown partridge.
WING: Gray mallard quill sections tied on sides of body and extending rearward half of body length.
ANTENNAE: Two wood duck flank feather fibers tied back long over body.
HEAD: Medium-brown dubbing fur.
NOTE: A prototype for many similar pupal imitations tied in various colors and sizes.
DIFFICULTY: 3.   SPECIES: All trout, LLS, SMB, PF.

QUILL GORDON

HOOK: Mustad 3906, sizes 10-16.
THREAD: Gray nylon, 6/0.
TAIL: Wood duck flank feather fibers.
BODY: Stripped peacock herl.
RIBBING: Fine gold wire.
HACKLE: Medium blue-dun (gray).
WING: Wood duck flank feather fibers.
NOTE: When dressing wet flies to simulate emerging insects, you might try using lighter-wire hooks, such as Mustad's 94840 or 94833, so the fly rides higher in the water.
DIFFICULTY: 2.   SPECIES: All trout, LLS, SMB, PF.

WOOLLY WORM

HOOK: Mustad 79580, sizes 2-16.
THREAD: Black nylon, 6/0.
TAIL: Red hackle fibers.
BODY: Black chenille.
RIBBING: Grizzly hackle.
WING: None.
NOTE: A very old European pattern, modernized by the late Don Martinez in the 1940s. Tied with variously colored chenille bodies.
DIFFICULTY: 1.   SPECIES: All trout, LLS, ST, LMB, SMB, PF.

 **LITTLE MARRYAT**

 **LIGHT CAHILL**

 **MARCH BROWN**

 **PARTRIDGE AND ORANGE**

 **PICKET PIN**

 **TAN CADDIS PUPA**

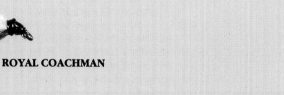 **ROYAL COACHMAN**

 **QUILL GORDON**

TELLICO

 **WOOLLY WORM**

(Flies shown 2.4 times actual size.)

ATHERTON MEDIUM

HOOK: Mustad 9671, sizes 12-16.
THREAD: Brown nylon, 6/0.
TAIL: Three ring-necked pheasant tail fibers.
ABDOMEN: Hare's-mask dubbing.
RIBBING: Fine gold oval tinsel.
WINGCASE: Goose or duck quill section dyed medium blue.
THORAX: Hare's-mask dubbing.
HACKLE: Brown partridge.
NOTE: A contemporary version of the pattern given by the late John Atherton in his 1951 book *The Fly and the Fish*.
DIFFICULTY: 2.   SPECIES: All trout, LLS, SMB, PF.

HENDRICKSON

HOOK: Mustad 9671, sizes 12-16.
THREAD: Brown nylon, 6/0.
TAIL: Wood duck flank feather fibers.
ABDOMEN: Grayish brown dubbing fur or blend.
RIBBING: Fine oval gold tinsel.
WINGCASE: Gray duck quill section.
THORAX: Grayish brown dubbing fur or blend.
HACKLE: Brown partridge.
DIFFICULTY: 2.   SPECIES: All trout, LLS, SMB, PF.

LITTLE YELLOW STONEFLY

HOOK: Mustad 9672, sizes 8-16.
THREAD: Yellow nylon, 6/0.
TAIL: Two yellow-dyed stripped goose fibers.
BODY: Amber dubbing fur or blend.
WINGCASE: Light mottled turkey quill section.
HACKLE: Pale ginger.
DIFFICULTY: 2.   SPECIES: All trout, LLS, SMB, PF.

GOLD-RIBBED HARE'S EAR

HOOK: Mustad 9671, sizes 12-16.
THREAD: Brown nylon, 6/0.
TAIL: Brown hackle fibers.
ABDOMEN: Hare's-mask dubbing.
RIBBING: Fine oval gold tinsel.
WINGCASE: Gray mallard quill section.
THORAX: Hare's-mask dubbing.
HACKLE: Dubbing fibers plucked outward from thorax.
DIFFICULTY: 2.   SPECIES: All trout, LLS, SMB, PF.

GRAY SHRIMP

HOOK: Mustad 3906, sizes 10-16.
THREAD: Gray nylon, 6/0.
TAIL: None.
SHELL: Strip of clear plastic-bag material tied in at rear of hook, pulled forward over body, and tied down at head.
BODY: Gray-olive dubbing fur blend, shaggy.
RIBBING: Fine oval gold tinsel.
HACKLE: Tufts of dubbing fur plucked outward on underside of body.
DIFFICULTY: 2.   SPECIES: All trout.

BITCH CREEK

HOOK: Mustad 79580, sizes 4-10.
THREAD: Black nylon, 6/0.
TAIL: Two white rubber hackle pieces.
ABDOMEN: Orange chenille colored top and sides with black waterproof marker.

THORAX: Black chenille.
HACKLE: Brown, wound through thorax.
ANTENNAE: Two strands white rubber hackle.
NOTE: The bicolored abdomen is commonly woven of black-and-orange chenille, but the waterproof marker method, suggested by Eric Leiser, is much simpler.
DIFFICULTY: 2.   SPECIES: All trout, LLS, SMB, PF.

ISONYCHIA

HOOK: Mustad 9671, sizes 12-16.
THREAD: Brown nylon, 6/0.
TAIL: Three peacock herl fibers, tied short.
ABDOMEN: Dark purplish brown dubbing fur or blend.
RIBBING: Dark brown thread.
STRIPE: Light moose mane fiber tied in at tail, pulled over body, and held down with ribbing.
WINGCASE: Dark mallard quill section.
THORAX: Dark purplish brown dubbing fur or blend.
HACKLE: Brown partridge.
NOTE: These nymphs are very active swimmers, so fish the imitation like a small bucktail or streamer.
DIFFICULTY: 3.   SPECIES: All trout, LLS.

LITTLE BLACK STONEFLY

HOOK: Mustad 9672, sizes 10-16.
THREAD: Black nylon, 6/0.
TAIL: Two black-dyed stripped goose fibers.
BODY: Black dubbing fur.
WINGCASE: Black goose or duck quill section.
HACKLE: Black.
ANTENNAE: Two black-dyed stripped goose fibers.
NOTE: In the last 15 years or so, numerous stonefly nymph patterns have been developed, many of them complicated. For a complete treatment, see *Stoneflies for the Angler* by Robert Boyle and Eric Leiser (Nick Lyons Books, New York).
DIFFICULTY: 2.   SPECIES: All trout, LLS, SMB, PF.

GREEN DRAKE (Western)

HOOK: Mustad 9671, sizes 8-16.
THREAD: Olive nylon, 6/0.
TAIL: Partridge hackle fibers dyed dark olive.
ABDOMEN: Dark-olive-dyed rabbit dubbing.
RIBBING: Heavy, dark brown thread.
WINGCASE: Black-dyed duck quill section.
THORAX: Same as abdomen.
HACKLE: Partridge hackle dyed dark olive.
NOTE: Modified version of a pattern by Al Troth, one of the West's most innovative and influential tiers. Useful in a variety of sizes; the natural is usually a size 8 or 10.
DIFFICULTY: 2.   SPECIES: All trout, LLS, SMB, PF.

LIGHT CAHILL

HOOK: Mustad 9671, sizes 12-16.
THREAD: Cream nylon, 6/0.
TAIL: Wood duck flank feather fibers.
ABDOMEN: Cream dubbing fur.
WINGCASE: Wood duck flank feather fibers.
HACKLE: Cream.
DIFFICULTY: 2.   SPECIES: All trout, LLS, SMB, PF.

ATHERTON MEDIUM

BITCH CREEK

HENDRICKSON

ISONYCHIA

LITTLE YELLOW STONEFLY

LITTLE BLACK STONEFLY

GOLD-RIBBED HARE'S EAR

GREEN DRAKE (Western)

GRAY SHRIMP

LIGHT CAHILL

(Flies shown 2.3 times actual size.)

NYMPHS

MARCH BROWN
HOOK: Mustad 9671, sizes 12-16.
THREAD: Brown nylon, 6/0.
TAIL: Three ring-necked pheasant tail fibers.
ABDOMEN: Tan dubbing fur or blend.
RIBBING: Brown thread.
WINGCASE: Ring-necked pheasant tail fibers.
THORAX: Tan dubbing fur or blend.
HACKLE: Brown partridge.
DIFFICULTY: 2.   SPECIES: All trout, LLS, SMB, PF.

MUSKRAT
HOOK: Mustad 9671, sizes 12-16.
THREAD: Black nylon, 6/0.
TAIL: None.
BODY: Gray muskrat dubbing fur.
HACKLE: Guinea hen hackle fibers.
HEAD: Black ostrich herl.
NOTE: This pattern is generally attributed to Polly Rosborough of Oregon, and Eric Leiser tells me it's America's best-selling nymph pattern. It's certainly easy to make and effective on all trout waters.
DIFFICULTY: 1.   SPECIES: All trout, LLS, SMB, PF.

PHEASANT TAIL
HOOK: Mustad 9671, sizes 12-16.
THREAD: Brown nylon, 6/0.
TAIL: Three ring-necked pheasant tail fibers.
ABDOMEN: Pheasant tail fibers wrapped around shank.
RIBBING: Fine gold or copper wire.
WINGCASE: Pheasant tail fibers pulled forward over thorax and tied down.
THORAX: Ring-necked pheasant tail fibers wound more fully than for abdomen.
HACKLE: Brown partridge.
NOTE: An adaptation of Frank Sawyer's classic British pattern, which calls for the body fibers to be wound together with copper wire and omits the hackle.
DIFFICULTY: 2.   SPECIES: All trout, LLS, SMB, PF.

QUILL GORDON
HOOK: Mustad 9671, sizes 12-16.
THREAD: Brown nylon, 6/0.
TAIL: Wood duck flank feather fibers.
ABDOMEN: Tan dubbing fur.
WINGCASE: Medium-gray duck quill section.
THORAX: Tan dubbing mixed with hare's-mask dubbing fur.
HACKLE: Light brown partridge.
DIFFICULTY: 2.   SPECIES: All trout.

ZUG BUG
HOOK: Mustad 9671, sizes 12-16.
THREAD: Olive nylon, 6/0.
TAIL: Three peacock sword fibers.
BODY: Peacock herl.
RIBBING: Fine oval silver tinsel.
WINGCASE: Trimmed tip of mallard flank feather tied in at head.
HACKLE: Brown.
DIFFICULTY: 2.   SPECIES: All trout, LLS, SMB, PF.

MONTANA
HOOK: Mustad 9672, sizes 6-12.
THREAD: Black nylon, 6/0.
TAIL: Black hackle fibers.
THORAX: Two strands fine black chenille wound together.
WINGCASE: Two strands black chenille pulled forward over thorax and tied down.
THORAX: Yellow chenille.
HACKLE: Black, wound through thorax.
NOTE: Using two strands of chenille side by side for the wingcase gives a wider and flatter wingcase than if just one larger strand were used.
DIFFICULTY: 1.   SPECIES: All trout, LLS, SMB, PF.

MARTINEZ
HOOK: Mustad 9671, sizes 12-16.
THREAD: Black nylon, 6/0.
TAIL: Guinea hen hackle fibers.
ABDOMEN: Black dubbing fur.
RIBBING: Fine oval gold tinsel.
WINGCASE: Duck or goose quill section dyed medium blue.
THORAX: Black dubbing fur.
HACKLE: Natural gray partridge.
NOTE: The wingcase on this pattern is sometimes made with a medium-green quill section instead of blue.
DIFFICULTY: 2.   SPECIES: All trout, LLS, SMB, PF.

PRINCE
HOOK: Mustad 9671, sizes 12-16.
THREAD: Black nylon, 6/0.
TAIL: Two fibers of brown stripped goose.
BODY: Peacock herl.
RIBBING: Fine oval gold tinsel.
HACKLE: Brown.
WING: Two white stripped goose fibers.
NOTE: I've included smallmouth bass on the species list for many of these trout flies since these bass often are found in similar river environments and feed very much like trout. Trout flies are often neglected for smallmouths but can be wonderfully effective.
DIFFICULTY: 2.   SPECIES: All trout, LLS, SMB, PF.

SQUIRREL HAIR
HOOK: Mustad 9671, sizes 12-16.
THREAD: Black nylon, 6/0.
TAIL: Gray squirrel guard hair.
ABDOMEN: Red squirrel body fur dubbing.
RIBBING: Fine oval gold tinsel.
THORAX: Gray squirrel body hair dubbing, tied rough.
NOTE: One version of a pattern popularized by Dave Whitlock in recent years, which I've used successfully all over the country, including the tailwater trout fisheries of Arkansas where the pattern is especially effective.
DIFFICULTY: 1.   SPECIES: All trout, LLS, SMB, PF.

TED'S STONEFLY
HOOK: Mustad 9672, sizes 6-12.
THREAD: Black nylon, 6/0.
TAIL: Two brown stripped goose fibers.
ABDOMEN: Brown chenille.
WINGCASE: Brown chenille.
THORAX: Orange chenille.
HACKLE: Brown hackle wound through thorax.
DIFFICULTY: 1.   SPECIES: All trout, LLS, SMB, PF.

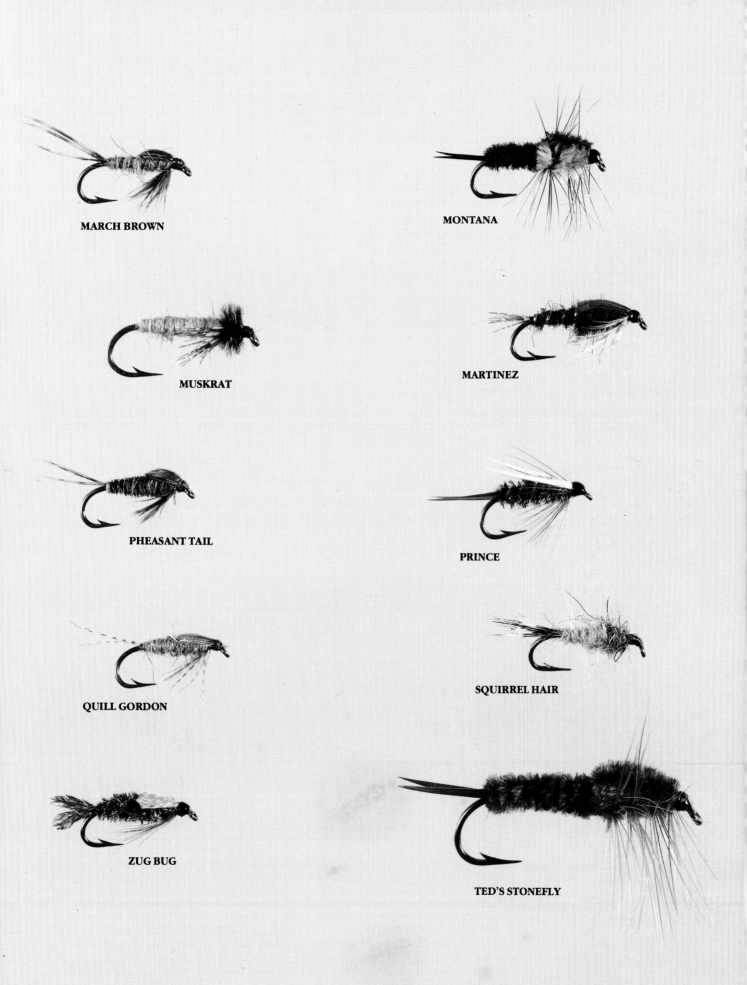

MARCH BROWN

MONTANA

MUSKRAT

MARTINEZ

PHEASANT TAIL

PRINCE

QUILL GORDON

SQUIRREL HAIR

ZUG BUG

TED'S STONEFLY

(Flies shown 2.3 times actual size.)

BLACK NOSE DACE

HOOK: Mustad 9575, sizes 2-10.
THREAD: Black nylon, 6/0.
TAIL: Red wool yarn, tied short.
BODY: Flat or embossed silver tinsel.
WING: White bucktail under either black-bear guard-hair fibers or black-dyed bucktail, topped with natural brown bucktail. Fly should be sparse, meaning no more than 6-10 strands of each color hair.
NOTE: Art Flick's famous pattern in which he originally used polar bear hair (no longer available) in the underwing.
DIFFICULTY: 2.   SPECIES: All trout, LLS, SMB, PF.

DARK EDSON TIGER

HOOK: Mustad 9575, sizes 2-10.
THREAD: Black nylon, 6/0.
TAG: Narrow flat gold tinsel.
TAIL: Yellow hackle fibers.
BODY: Yellow chenille (medium size).
WING: Brown bucktail dyed yellow.
HACKLE: Yellow, tied as a beard.
CHEEKS: Jungle cock or substitute, optional.
NOTE: Both the bucktail for this fly and the yellow bucktail needed for the Light Edson Tiger come from a natural bucktail dyed yellow.
DIFFICULTY: 2.   SPECIES: All trout, LLS, SMB, PF.

BLACK-AND-WHITE

HOOK: Mustad 9575, sizes 2-10.
THREAD: Black nylon, 6/0.
TAIL: Red bucktail fibers.
BODY: Embossed silver tinsel.
WING: Black over white bucktail.
NOTE: Sometimes called Esopus Bucktail, after a famous Catskill river that often runs cloudy because of a reservoir's discharge. Black flies are especially effective in off-color water, which probably accounts for the association between the Esopus and this pattern.
DIFFICULTY: 1.   SPECIES: All trout, LLS, SMB.

LLAMA

HOOK: Mustad 79580, sizes 6-10.
THREAD: Black nylon, 6/0.
TAIL: Grizzly hackle fibers.
RIBBING: Flat silver tinsel.
BODY: Red floss.
WING: Woodchuck guard hairs.
HACKLE: Grizzly wound as a collar and tied back.
NOTE: Popularized in recent years by Eric Leiser, this pattern sometimes features a white-painted eye with black pupil.
DIFFICULTY: 2.   SPECIES: All trout, LLS, SMB, PF.

LIGHT EDSON TIGER

HOOK: Mustad 9575, sizes 2-10.
THREAD: Yellow nylon, 6/0.
TAG: Fine flat gold tinsel.
TAIL: Black-and-white tipped wood duck.
BODY: Peacock herl.
WING: Yellow bucktail.
TOPPING: Dyed red hackle fibers, 1/3 of wing length.
DIFFICULTY: 2.   SPECIES: All trout, LLS, SMB, PF.

MICKEY FINN

HOOK: Mustad 9575, sizes 2-10.
THREAD: Black nylon, 6/0.
TAIL: None.
BODY: Flat silver tinsel.
RIBBING: Oval silver tinsel.
WING: Yellow bucktail under red bucktail topped with yellow bucktail. The top bunch of yellow should be equal in bulk to the lower bunches of red and yellow combined.
NOTE: Popularized by the late John Alden Knight during the 1940s. A common tying fault is using too much material in the wing.
DIFFICULTY: 2.   SPECIES: All trout, LLS, P, NP, SMB, LMB, PF.

ROYAL COACHMAN

HOOK: Mustad 9575, sizes 2-10.
THREAD: Black nylon, 6/0.
TAIL: Golden pheasant tippet fibers.
BODY: Back to front: peacock herl, red floss, peacock herl.
WING: White bucktail.
HACKLE: Brown wound as a collar and tied back.
NOTE: See notes on body construction for Spruce streamers.
DIFFICULTY: 3.   SPECIES: All trout, LLS, SMB, PF.

SQUIRREL TAIL

HOOK: Mustad 9575, sizes 6-10.
THREAD: Black nylon, 6/0.
TAIL: Red wool yarn tied short.
BODY: Flat silver tinsel.
WING: Gray squirrel tail fibers.
NOTE: See tying directions on page 10.
DIFFICULTY: 1.   SPECIES: All trout, LLS, SMB, PF.

WARDEN'S WORRY

HOOK: Mustad 9575, sizes 2-10.
THREAD: Black nylon, 6/0.
TAIL: Red duck quill section.
RIBBING: Flat silver tinsel.
BODY: Yellowish orange dubbing or wool.
WING: Brown bucktail.
HACKLE: Yellow.
NOTE: Some versions call for yellow-orange-dyed hare's-ear dubbing, which will produce a more lifelike fly.
DIFFICULTY: 2.   SPECIES: All trout, LLS, SMB, PF.

ZONKER

HOOK: Mustad 9674, sizes 2-6.
THREAD: Black nylon, 6/0.
BODY: Silver Mylar tubing.
WING: Natural brown rabbit fur on a ⅛-inch-wide strip cut from a tanned hide.
HACKLE: Grizzly.
NOTE: Slide tubing over hook and tie down at bend. Tie down rear end of wing in the same spot and whip-finish. Tie down front end of tubing behind head, pull wing forward, and tie down rabbit strip in the same spot, trimming excess. Some versions call for a flat metal underbody folded over the shank and trimmed to a deep body shape, which shapes the tubing then slipped over it. Various color combinations popular, including white, yellow, and black.
DIFFICULTY: 4.   SPECIES: All trout, LLS, LMB, SMB.

BLACK NOSE DACE

MICKEY FINN

DARK EDSON TIGER

ROYAL COACHMAN

BLACK-AND-WHITE

SQUIRREL TAIL

LLAMA

WARDEN'S WORRY

LIGHT EDSON TIGER

ZONKER

(Flies shown 1.6 times actual size.)

BADGER MATUKA
HOOK: Mustad 9575, sizes 2-10.
THREAD: Brown nylon, 6/0.
TAIL: None.
BODY: Cream wool yarn or dubbing with a little red wool or dubbing behind head.
RIBBING: Fine oval gold tinsel.
WING: Four badger hackles tied down Matuka-style.
HACKLE: Badger, wound as a collar and tied back.
NOTE: Tie in wing as per conventional streamer, then wind ribbing forward over body and through wing fibers to bind wing to body. To prevent twisting when winding ribbing, make the first forward turn so the ribbing binds the hackles to the body and not the bare hook. Try other colors, especially olive.
DIFFICULTY: 5. SPECIES: All trout, LLS, LMB, SMB, PF.

BALLOU SPECIAL
HOOK: Mustad 9575, sizes 2-10
THREAD: Black nylon, 6/0.
TAIL: Golden pheasant crest.
BODY: Flat silver tinsel.
WING: Small (about 8-10 fibers) bunch red bucktail under white marabou. Top with 6-8 strands of peacock herl.
NOTE: Make bucktail underwing slightly shorter than marabou, which in turn should be slightly shorter than herl topping. Jungle cock cheeks are traditional but can be omitted.
DIFFICULTY: 2. SPECIES: All trout, SS, LLS, LMB, SMB, PF.

BARNES SPECIAL
HOOK: Mustad 9575, sizes 2-10.
THREAD: Red nylon, 6/0.
TAIL: Section of duck quill dyed red.
BODY: Flat silver tinsel.
RIBBING: Medium oval silver tinsel.
WING: Red bucktail (6-10 fibers) under white bucktail (6-10 fibers). Then two yellow saddle hackles under two grizzly saddle hackles.
HACKLE: White hackle wound as a collar and tied back.
NOTE: Some versions of this pattern omit the tail entirely, while others call variously for silver pheasant, jungle fowl body feathers, or black hackle tips.
DIFFICULTY: 3. SPECIES: All trout, LLS, SMB, PF.

BLACK GHOST
HOOK: Mustad 9575, sizes 2-10.
THREAD: Black nylon, 6/0.
TAIL: Yellow hackle fibers.
RIBBING: Flat silver tinsel.
BODY: Black floss or wool yarn.
WING: Four white saddle hackles.
HACKLE: Yellow, tied as a beard and same length as tail fibers.
NOTE: Foregoing is the traditional version. Try also with white marabou for wing and yellow marabou for tail and throat hackle.
DIFFICULTY: 2. SPECIES: All trout, LLS, LMB, SMB, PF.

BLACK ANGUS
HOOK: Mustad 79580, sizes 2-8.
THREAD: Black nylon, 6/0.
TAIL: Four black saddle hackles extending one shank length past hook bend.
BODY: Black floss tapered over lead-wire underbody. Wind lead wire on forward half of shank only.
RIBBING: Black marabou tied in by the feather tip at end of body and palmered forward. Stroke fibers to the rear while winding forward.
HEAD: Black deerhair spun and trimmed Muddler-style.

NOTE: Developed by my friend Eric Leiser for big Alaskan rainbows, this pattern is excellent in a variety of sizes for all species of both trout and bass.
DIFFICULTY: 5. SPECIES: All trout, LMB, SMB.

BLACK WOOLLY BUGGER
HOOK: Mustad 79580, sizes 2-12.
THREAD: Black nylon, 6/0.
TAIL: Black marabou, almost as long as hook shank.
RIBBING: Black saddle hackle palmered forward over body.
BODY: Black chenille.
NOTE: Tied in various color combinations, this is the most popular. Sometimes weighted, sometimes with a few Flashabou strands added to tail.
DIFFICULTY: 2. SPECIES: All trout, LLS, LMB, SMB, PF.

BLACK-STRIPED MINNOW
HOOK: Mustad 9575, sizes 2-10.
THREAD: Brown nylon, 6/0.
TAIL: Section from white-tipped wood duck flank feather.
BODY: Flat silver tinsel.
WING: Sparse white bucktail under sparse brown bucktail. One badger saddle hackle full length on each side of hair wing.
HACKLE: Orange hackle fibers tied as beard.
NOTE: An old favorite of mine adapted slightly from Larry Koller's 1950 book *Taking Larger Trout*. This pattern does just what the book title implies but is seldom found in other pattern books.
DIFFICULTY: 3. SPECIES: All trout.

CHIEF NEEDAHBEH
HOOK: Mustad 9575, sizes 2-10.
THREAD: Black nylon, 6/0.
TAIL: Red duck or goose quill section.
TAG: Fine silver tinsel.
BODY: Red floss.
RIBBING: Fine silver tinsel.
WING: Two red saddle hackles with one yellow saddle hackle on each side.
HACKLE: Red, wound and tied back.
NOTE: Chief Nedahba (the correct spelling, as opposed to the popularized version in the fly name) was a Penobscot (Maine) Indian and a crony of Bill Edson's (of Light and Dark Tiger fame) in Maine during the 1930s.
DIFFICULTY: 2. SPECIES: All trout, LLS, SMB.

DARK SPRUCE
HOOK: Mustad 9575, sizes 2-10.
THREAD: Black nylon, 6/0.
TAIL: Six peacock sword fibers.
BODY: Rear half: red floss; forward half: peacock herl.
WING: Four furnace hackles.
HACKLE: Furnace, wound as a collar and tied back.
NOTE: A popular fly for fall-run brown trout from Maine to California.
DIFFICULTY: 3. SPECIES: All trout, LLS, SMB, PF.

DARK HORNBERG
HOOK: Mustad 9671, sizes 6-16.
THREAD: Brown nylon, 6/0.
TAIL: None.
BODY: Dubbing: dark olive-brown hare's-ear blend.
WING: A few strands of brown bucktail or calftail with bronze mallard flank feathers tied flat along shank on either side.
HACKLE: Brown and blue-dun mixed, tied as a dry-fly collar.
NOTE: Sometimes fished as a dry fly in smaller sizes.
DIFFICULTY: 3. SPECIES: All trout, LLS, SMB, PF.

BADGER MATUKA

BLACK WOOLLY BUGGER

BALLOU SPECIAL

BLACK-STRIPED MINNOW

BARNES SPECIAL

CHIEF NEEDAHBEH

BLACK GHOST

DARK SPRUCE

BLACK ANGUS

DARK HORNBERG

(Flies shown 1.4 times actual size.)

GOLDEN DEMON

HOOK: Mustad 9575, sizes 6-10.
THREAD: Black nylon, 6/0.
TAIL: Golden pheasant crest.
BODY: Flat gold tinsel.
WING: Bronze mallard flank.
HACKLE: Hot orange.
DIFFICULTY: 2.   SPECIES: BkT (and all trout), LLS.

GRAY GHOST

HOOK: Mustad 9575, sizes 2-10.
THREAD: Gray nylon, 6/0.
TAIL: None.
RIBBING: Medium flat silver tinsel.
BODY: Orange floss.
THROAT: Golden pheasant crest, tied in shank length and curving upward toward body, below which is a slightly longer bunch of white bucktail, sparse.
WING: Four light dun (gray) saddle hackles, with three to four strands peacock herl as a topping.
SHOULDERS: Silver pheasant body feathers, one each side of wing and 1/3 body length.
CHEEKS: Jungle cock or substitute, optional.
NOTE: Developed in the 1920s by Carrie Stevens of Upper Dam, Maine, this is a smelt imitation. Smelt are a long, slim baitfish, and your dressing should reflect that shape. This dressing is traditional, of which the illustrated pattern is a slight variation.
DIFFICULTY: 4.   SPECIES: BkT (and all trout), LLS.

HORNBERG

HOOK: Mustad 9671, sizes 6-16.
THREAD: Black nylon, 6/0.
TAIL: None.
BODY: Flat silver tinsel.
WING: Sparse yellow bucktail with mallard flank feather tied flat on either side.
HACKLE: Brown and grizzly mixed as a dry-fly collar.
CHEEKS: Jungle cock or substitute, optional.
DIFFICULTY: 2.   SPECIES: All trout, LLS, SMB, PF.

JOE'S SMELT

HOOK: Mustad 9575, sizes 2-8.
THREAD: Red nylon, 6/0.
TAIL: Red hackle or hair fibers, tied short.
TAG: Red thread used to tie off rear end of Mylar tubing.
BODY: Woven Mylar tubing—cut to length, remove core, and slide over hook shank to form body. Bind down both ends with red thread.
WING: Narrow mallard flank feather tied flat and extending to tail.
HEAD: Lacquered black with yellow eye.
NOTE: Landlocked salmon, for which this pattern was developed, are notorious for nipping at the end of a streamer fly, so make sure your wings on this pattern aren't too long.
DIFFICULTY: 2.   SPECIES: BkT, LLS.

LIGHT SPRUCE

HOOK: Mustad 9575, sizes 2-10.
THREAD: Black nylon, 6/0.
TAIL: Six peacock sword fibers.
BODY: Rear half: red floss; forward half: peacock herl.
WING: Four badger saddle hackles.
HACKLE: Badger hackle wound as a collar and tied back.
NOTE: One way to make this body is to tie floss and herl fibers in at midshank. Wind thread to head position. Wind floss to rear and then forward to head position. Wind herl forward over floss on front half of body.
DIFFICULTY: 3.   SPECIES: All trout, LLS, SMB, PF.

MUDDLER MINNOW

HOOK: Mustad 79580, sizes 2-12.
THREAD: Black Monocord, 3/0.
TAIL: Mottled turkey quill, tied in so fibers curve upward.
BODY: Flat gold tinsel.
WING: Sparse gray squirrel tail, under two sections of mottled turkey quill sections (tied in wet-fly style so fibers curve downward toward tail).
HEAD: Light brown deerhair spun and clipped to shape.
NOTE: Fish as a dry, wet, nymph, or streamer—this may be the world's most versatile recognized fly pattern. See tying directions on page 9.
DIFFICULTY: 5.   SPECIES: All trout, LLS, ST, AS, LMB, SMB, PF.

NEXT-TO-NOTHING

HOOK: Mustad 9575, sizes 6-10.
THREAD: Black nylon, 6/0.
WING: Two badger saddle hackles, one on each side of hook shank.
NOTE: This is no joke. Generically, it's one of the oldest types of artificial flies. Badger hackle looks like a minnow in the water, and the action you impart to the fly will bring the strikes.
DIFFICULTY: 1.   SPECIES: All trout, LLS, SMB.

NINE-THREE

HOOK: Mustad 9575, sizes 2-10.
THREAD: Black nylon, 6/0.
TAIL: None.
BODY: Flat silver tinsel.
WING: Sparse white bucktail (8-10 fibers) under two green black saddle hackles. Two green saddle hackles tied over the black.
DIFFICULTY: 2.   SPECIES: All trout, LLS, SMB.

SUPERVISOR

HOOK: Mustad 9575, sizes 2-10.
THREAD: Black nylon, 6/0.
TAIL: Red wool yarn tied short.
BODY: Flat silver tinsel.
RIBBING: Medium oval silver tinsel.
WING: Sparse (8-10 fibers) white bucktail under four light-blue-dyed saddle hackles. Use three to four strands peacock herl for topping.
SHOULDERS: One green saddle hackle 2/3 as long as and on each side of the blue.
NOTE: Another classic smelt imitation; use only two blue saddles for a slimmer profile.
DIFFICULTY: 3.   SPECIES: All trout, LLS, SMB, PF.

WHITE MARABOU MUDDLER

HOOK: Mustad 79580, sizes 2-8.
THREAD: White Monocord, 3/0.
TAIL: Red fluff from base of hackle feather.
BODY: Braided Flashabou, sometimes over lead wire.
WING: White marabou with a few strands of silver Krystal Flash and topped by a few strands of peacock herl.
HEAD: Deerhair spun and trimmed to shape with hair-fiber collar left untrimmed.
NOTE: A good "locator" pattern—when a big trout flashes at the fly but doesn't hit, switch to a more imitative streamer pattern and try the same fish again.
DIFFICULTY: 5.   SPECIES: All trout, LLS, SMB, LMB.

GOLDEN DEMON

MUDDLER MINNOW

GRAY GHOST

NEXT-TO-NOTHING

HORNBERG

NINE-THREE

JOE'S SMELT

SUPERVISOR

LIGHT SPRUCE

WHITE MARABOU MUDDLER

(Flies shown 1.4 times actual size.)

BRAD'S BRAT

HOOK: Mustad 9049, sizes 4-10.
THREAD: Black nylon, 6/0.
TAG: Fine gold tinsel.
TAIL: Bucktail fibers, white over orange.
BODY: Orange wool for rear half; front half red.
HACKLE: Brown.
WING: Bucktail, white over orange.
NOTE: Named for the late Enos Bradner, a writer and angler who helped pioneer fly fishing for Northwestern steelhead.
DIFFICULTY: 2. SPECIES: ST, AS.

COMET

HOOK: Mustad 9049, sizes 4-10.
THREAD: Red nylon, 6/0.
TAIL: Orange calftail, long.
BODY: Silver tinsel.
HACKLE: Yellow and orange mixed.
EYES: Nickel-plated lead eyes.
NOTE: One of many comet patterns tied in this style, often with oval tinsel instead of flat, and traditionally with eyes made of bead-chain instead of the newer (1987) lead eyes.
DIFFICULTY: 2. SPECIES: ST.

FALL FAVORITE

HOOK: Mustad 9049, sizes 4-10.
THREAD: Red nylon, 6/0.
TAIL: None.
BODY: Embossed silver tinsel.
HACKLE: Red.
WING: Bright orange bucktail or equivalent.
NOTE: Embossed silver tinsel is more reflective but available only in metal. Your regular, more easily used flat Mylar will also work.
DIFFICULTY: 1. SPECIES: ST, AS.

McCLEOD'S UGLY

HOOK: Mustad 9049, sizes 4-10.
THREAD: Black nylon, 6/0.
TAIL: Fluffy fibers from base of orange feather.
BODY: Black chenille.
RIBBING: Grizzly hackle.
WING: Black bucktail or equivalent.
HACKLE: Grizzly.
NOTE: A favorite steelhead fly, famous for taking 30-pound-plus steelhead in northern British Columbia.
DIFFICULTY: 2. SPECIES: ST.

ORANGE DEMON

HOOK: Mustad 9049, sizes 4-10.
THREAD: Orange nylon, 6/0.
TAIL: Orange hackle fibers.
BODY: Fluorescent yellow wool.
HACKLE: Orange.
WING: Black calftail or equivalent.
NOTE: I've taken both Northwestern steelhead and Northeastern Atlantic salmon on this pattern, so of course it's a favorite.
DIFFICULTY: 1. SPECIES: ST, AS.

PURPLE PERIL

HOOK: Mustad 9049, sizes 4-10.
THREAD: Black nylon, 6/0.
TAG: Fine silver tinsel.
TAIL: Purple hackle fibers.
BODY: Purple chenille.
RIBBING: Silver tinsel.
HACKLE: Purple.
WING: Black calftail or equivalent.
NOTE: I use "equivalent" black hair for these patterns to mean black bear, black bucktail, black squirrel tail, or black calftail. They all work.
DIFFICULTY: 2. SPECIES: ST, AS.

SKUNK

HOOK: Mustad 9049, sizes 4-10.
THREAD: Black nylon, 6/0.
TAIL: Red hackle fibers.
BODY: Black chenille.
RIBBING: Silver tinsel.
HACKLE: Black.
WING: White calftail or equivalent.
NOTE: Perhaps the most popular steelhead pattern. I've specified a Mustad low-water salmon hook for these patterns. Many people use the heavier, faster-sinking, Mustad 36890 salmon hook.
DIFFICULTY: 2. SPECIES: ST.

SPRING WIGGLER

HOOK: Mustad 9049, sizes 4-10.
THREAD: Brown nylon, 6/0.
TAIL: Fox (red) squirrel tail fibers.
BODY: Orange or tan chenille.
RIBBING: Grizzly hackle.
WING: Continuation of tail fibers pulled forward over body and tied down at head.
NOTE: The only specifically midwestern pattern in this series, used commonly for Michigan steelhead.
DIFFICULTY: 2. SPECIES: ST.

SKYKOMISH SUNRISE

HOOK: Mustad 9049, sizes 4-10.
THREAD: Red nylon, 6/0.
TAIL: Red and yellow hackle fibers mixed.
BODY: Red chenille.
RIBBING: Silver tinsel.
HACKLE: Red and yellow mixed.
WING: White calftail or equivalent.
NOTE: Equivalent white winging includes calftail, bucktail, and monga.
DIFFICULTY: 2. SPECIES: ST.

SILVER HILTON

HOOK: Mustad 9049, sizes 4-10.
THREAD: Black nylon, 6/0.
TAIL: Mallard flank fibers.
BODY: Black chenille.
RIBBING: Silver tinsel.
HACKLE: Grizzly.
WING: Two grizzly hackle tips.
NOTE: Tie in the hackle-tip wings "back to back" so they curve outward giving more action in the water.
DIFFICULTY: 2. SPECIES: ST.

BRAD'S BRAT

COMET

FALL FAVORITE

McCLEOD'S UGLY

ORANGE DEMON

PURPLE PERIL

SKUNK

SPRING WIGGLER

SKYKOMISH SUNRISE

SILVER HILTON

(Flies shown 1.8 times actual size.)

BLACK BEAR GREEN BUTT

HOOK: Mustad 36890, sizes 4-10.
THREAD: Black nylon, 6/0.
TAG: Oval silver tinsel.
TAIL: Black hackle or black bear fibers.
BUTT: Fluorescent green wool.
BODY: Black wool.
RIBBING: Oval silver tinsel.
HACKLE: Black.
WING: Black bear hair fibers.
NOTE: Sometimes with black floss instead of wool and occasionally with a peacock herl body.
DIFFICULTY: 2. SPECIES: AS, ST.

BLUE CHARM

HOOK: Mustad 36890, sizes 4-10.
THREAD: Black nylon, 6/0.
TIP: Oval silver tinsel.
TAG: Yellow floss.
TAIL: Golden pheasant crest.
BODY: Black floss.
RIBBING: Oval silver tinsel.
HACKLE: Medium blue.
WING: Gray squirrel tail fibers.
DIFFICULTY: 3. SPECIES: AS.

COSSEBOOM

HOOK: Mustad 36890, sizes 4-10.
THREAD: Red nylon, 6/0.
TAG: Oval silver tinsel.
TAIL: Strand of medium olive floss.
BODY: Medium olive floss.
RIBBING: Oval silver tinsel.
HACKLE: Light yellow.
WING: Gray squirrel tail fibers.
NOTE: A favorite on Maine salmon rivers.
DIFFICULTY: 2. SPECIES: AS.

CROSSFIELD

HOOK: Mustad 36890, sizes 4-10.
THREAD: Black nylon, 6/0.
TIP: Oval silver tinsel.
TAG: Yellow floss.
TAIL: Golden pheasant crest.
BODY: Embossed silver tinsel.
HACKLE: Medium blue.
WING: Gray squirrel tail fibers.
DIFFICULTY: 2. SPECIES: AS.

ENGLE'S BUTTERFLY

HOOK: Mustad 36890, sizes 4-10.
THREAD: Black nylon, 6/0.
TIP: Oval silver tinsel.
TAG: Fluorescent green floss.
TAIL: Fine red duck quill section.
BODY: Peacock herl.
WING: Fine white hair (goat or calf) tied back at 45 degrees and divided.
HACKLE: Brown, wound dry-fly-style.
DIFFICULTY: 3. SPECIES: AS.

GREEN HIGHLANDER

HOOK: Mustad 36890, sizes 4-10.
THREAD: Black nylon, 6/0.
TAG: Yellow floss.
TIP: Oval silver tinsel.
TAIL: Golden pheasant crest under a short section of white-tipped wood duck flank.
BUTT: Black wool.

BODY: Rear 1/3: light yellow floss; forward 2/3: medium-green-dyed dubbing fur.
RIBBING: Oval silver tinsel.
BODY HACKLE: Green portion of body ribbed with medium green hackle (in addition to tinsel).
WING: From bottom to top: a few golden pheasant tippet fibers, then fine layers of yellow-, orange-, and green-dyed monga ringtail fibers, topped by a sparse bunch of red (fox) squirrel fibers, with two bright-orange-dyed small breast feathers tied as a topping at the head.
HACKLE: Medium yellow.
NOTE: The secret to this complicated pattern is not using too many turns of thread at any given step and not using too much of any one material.
DIFFICULTY: 5. SPECIES: AS.

HAIRY MARY

HOOK: Mustad 36890, sizes 4-10.
THREAD: Black nylon, 6/0.
TAG: Oval gold tinsel.
TAIL: Golden pheasant crest.
BODY: Black floss.
RIBBING: Oval gold tinsel.
HACKLE: Medium blue.
WING: Red (fox) squirrel.
NOTE: Having watched my friend Lou Black take a 30-pounder with this pattern on Norway's Gaula River last summer, I couldn't leave it out.
DIFFICULTY: 2. SPECIES: AS.

ORANGE BLOSSOM

HOOK: Mustad 36890, sizes 4-10.
THREAD: Black nylon, 6/0.
TIP: Oval silver tinsel.
TAG: Orange floss.
TAIL: Golden pheasant crest topped with a few golden pheasant tippet fibers dyed red.
BUTT: Black wool.
BODY: Embossed silver tinsel.
RIBBING: Medium yellow hackle.
WING: Brown and white bucktail mixed.
HACKLE: Orange.
DIFFICULTY: 3. SPECIES: AS.

ROGER'S FANCY

HOOK: Mustad 36890, sizes 4-10.
THREAD: Black nylon, 6/0.
TIP: Oval silver tinsel.
TAG: Yellow floss.
TAIL: Peacock sword feather fibers.
BODY: Green wool.
RIBBING: Oval silver tinsel.
HACKLE: Yellow under medium green.
WING: Gray fox guard-hair fibers.
DIFFICULTY: 2. SPECIES: AS.

RUSTY RAT

HOOK: Mustad 36890, sizes 4-10.
THREAD: Red nylon, 6/0.
TAG: Oval gold tinsel.
TAIL: Peacock sword feather fibers.
BODY: Rear half: golden yellow floss; front half: peacock herl. Section of floss folded back over rear of body.
HACKLE: Grizzly.
WING: Gray fox guard-hair fibers or black and white monga fibers mixed.
DIFFICULTY: 3. SPECIES: AS.

BLACK BEAR GREEN BUTT

GREEN HIGHLANDER

BLUE CHARM

HAIRY MARY

COSSEBOOM

ORANGE BLOSSOM

CROSSFIELD

ROGER'S FANCY

ENGLE'S BUTTERFLY

RUSTY RAT

(Flies shown 1.8 times actual size.)

BLUEFISH FLY
HOOK: Mustad 34007, sizes 3/0-2.
THREAD: Red nylon, 6/0.
TAIL: None.
BODY: None.
WING: White Fishair under a few strands of green Krystal Flash, topped with green Fishair. All tied in at rear of hook.
HEAD: Coated with clear epoxy.
NOTE: Bluefish have sharp teeth and will quickly destroy most flies. Lefty Kreh showed me this pattern about 12 years ago, and it's proved its durability with bluefish ever since.
DIFFICULTY: 1.   SPECIES: B, SB, PK, NP, WF, SST.

LEFTY'S DECEIVER
HOOK: Mustad 34007, sizes 3/0-2.
THREAD: White nylon, 6/0.
TAIL: Four to six white saddle hackles, long, and flanked on each side by a few strands of Flashabou or Krystal Flash, color to match topping.
BODY: Silver or pearlescent Mylar tinsel.
WING: White bucktail under hook, blue bucktail on top; both extending to hook bend. Peacock herl fibers over top wing.
HEAD: White, with painted eyes.
NOTE: Popularized by Lefty Kreh, this is currently the most popular all-around saltwater streamer pattern, often tied with various color combinations, including all white. I've used these flies successfully for everything from northern pike and striped bass to Mexican snook.
DIFFICULTY: 2.   SPECIES: Most saltwater gamefish, LMB, P, NP.

STU APTE TARPON FLY
HOOK: Mustad 34007, sizes 3/0-5/0.
THREAD: Red, 2/0 or "A" nylon.
TAIL: One orange saddle hackle over a yellow hackle on each side, tied to flare outward. Sometimes with Krystal Flash added between the hackles.
HACKLE: Orange and yellow (saddle hackle) mixed.
HEAD: Hook shank covered with red tying thread, then lacquered red. Painted eyes in front of hackle.
NOTE: Stu Apte, a former Pan American pilot, has established a variety of saltwater records, including several tarpon records, a sport that he helped to pioneer.
DIFFICULTY: 2.   SPECIES: TN, LMB, P, NP.

SIMPLE SAND EEL
HOOK: Mustad 34007, sizes 3/0-2.
THREAD: Olive Kevlar (about 3/0 in size).
TAIL: Long white bucktail, topped by green Krystal Flash, and flanked on each side with one long, thin olive-dyed saddle hackle.
BODY: None.
HEAD: Olive-dyed deerhair, spun and trimmed to shape, with a few fibers left as a hackle. Plastic doll eyes glued in with five-minute epoxy.
NOTE: My own pattern, which imitates a favorite striped bass food, is based on a tying style first shown me by Bill Catherwood of Massachusetts, a superb saltwater fly tier. The fly-dressing problem here is in producing flies large in bulk but streamlined and of little weight in casting, and deerhair is often a practical solution.
DIFFICULTY: 3.   SPECIES: SB, WF.

GIBBS STRIPER
HOOK: Mustad 34007, sizes 3/0-2.
THREAD: Black nylon, 6/0.
TAIL: None.
BODY: Flat silver tinsel.
WING: White bucktail, with a strip of blue-dyed goose quill extending on either side.
SHOULDER: Teal breast feather or other well-barred feather.
HEAD: Black, sometimes with painted eyes.
NOTE: Although U.S. saltwater fly fishing is more than 100 years old, there are very few traditional patterns. This is an older pattern developed for striped bass by Harold Gibbs of Rhode Island.
DIFFICULTY: 2.   SPECIES: SB, WF.

GLASS MINNOW
HOOK: Mustad 34007, sizes 2/0-2.
THREAD: Brown nylon, 6/0.
TAIL: None.
BODY: Clear plastic V-rib over silver tinsel.
WING: White bucktail under red squirrel tail, topped with a few strands of silver Flashabou.
HEAD: Brown with painted eyes.
NOTE: A generic saltwater minnow imitation, sometimes made with a white-and-green bucktail wing with Flashabou between the two wing colors.
DIFFICULTY: 2.   SPECIES: SB, WF, SST.

BONEFISH BUNNY
HOOK: Mustad 34007, sizes 4-8.
THREAD: Olive nylon, 6/0.
TAIL: None.
BODY: Olive chenille.
WING: Olive-dyed rabbit fur hide strip with fur attached.
NOTE: To tie: Make chenille body normally, then remove hook from vise. Use your bodkin to poke a hole in end of hide strip, then pass hook point through hole. Put hook back in vise inverted, pull hide strip forward firmly, and tie off at head. Try various color combinations.
DIFFICULTY: 1.   SPECIES: BF, PT.

CRAZY CHARLIE
HOOK: Mustad 34007, sizes 4-8.
THREAD: White nylon, 6/0.
TAIL: Silver Krystal Flash strands.
BODY: Clear V-rib plastic wound over silver tinsel.
WING: White calftail fibers under two white hackle tips.
HEAD: Silver bead-chain eyes tied on top of hook at head.
NOTE: Tied in various color combinations. Flashier bonefish patterns, this one especially, are also excellent shad flies.
DIFFICULTY: 2.   SPECIES: BF, SD.

TAN BONEFISH SPECIAL
HOOK: Mustad 34007, sizes 4-8.
THREAD: Red nylon, 6/0.
TAIL: Orange marabou.
BODY: Tan chenille.
WING: White bucktail, flanked by a grizzly hackle tip on each side.
HEAD: Red, with painted eyes.
NOTE: Adapted slightly from a pattern by Chico Fernandez, a well-known saltwater fly tier in south Florida.
DIFFICULTY: 2.   SPECIES: BF.

BLUEFISH FLY

LEFTY'S DECEIVER

STU APTE TARPON FLY

SIMPLE SAND EEL

GIBBS STRIPER

GLASS MINNOW

BONEFISH BUNNY

CRAZY CHARLIE

TAN BONEFISH SPECIAL

(Flies shown 1.2 times actual size.)

FEATHER EEL

HOOK: Mustad 37189, sizes 1/0-4.

THREAD: Black Monocord, 3/0.

TAIL: Three to five saddle hackles, tied long. Commonly natural grizzly or hackle dyed purple, yellow, or black. Flashabou or Krystal Flash optional.

BODY: Fur dubbing, wool yarn, or chenille to match hackle color. Monofilament weedguard optional.

HACKLE: Saddle hackle (color to match) wound over body and wound more fully at head.

HEAD: Bead-chain eyes or painted lead eyes.

NOTE: Fly fishing's answer to the plastic worm. Weighted eyes on top of the hook shank will make the hook ride upside down and vice versa. Take your pick.

DIFFICULTY: 2.   SPECIES: LMB, SMB.

RABBIT-FUR LEECH

HOOK: Mustad 37189, sizes 1/0-4.

THREAD: Purple nylon, 6/0.

TAIL: Thin purple-dyed rabbit hide strip with fur attached, long.

BODY/HACKLE: Thin purple-dyed rabbit fur strip tied in at tail and wound forward around shank to head.

HEAD: Painted lead or bead-chain eyes.

NOTE: Try various colors, including yellow, black, olive, and natural brown. Another "plastic worm" sort of fly that's easy to make.

DIFFICULTY: 2.   SPECIES: LMB, SMB.

BUBBLE PUP

HOOK: Mustad 37189, sizes 1/0-4.

THREAD: Yellow Monocord, 3/0.

TAIL: Two black hackles, tied to flare.

BODY/HEAD/HACKLE: Yellow-dyed deerhair, spun and tripped to shape, leaving tips of the rearmost bunch untrimmed as a hackle collar.

NOTE: Helen Shaw, a wonderful lady and superb fly tier, demonstrates this pattern in *Art Flick's Master Fly Tying Guide,* which you should see for tying detail. Trim the head face at a slant and coat the front surface with silicone sealer so the bug will chug and burble well on the surface.

DIFFICULTY: 4.   SPECIES: LMB, SMB.

BLACK/WHITE HAIRBUG

HOOK: Mustad 37189, sizes 1/0-4.

THREAD: Black Monocord, 3/0.

TAIL: Four black saddle hackles, two on each side, flaring apart.

HACKLE: Black.

BODY: Black deerhair, spun and trimmed, with white deerhair in front, bivisible style. Black rubber hackle tied in between black hair bunches.

NOTE: A generic deerhair bass bug, popularized in recent years by Dave Whitlock. Sometimes heavy monofilament is tied in at the tail and tied off at the head as a weedguard.

DIFFICULTY: 5.   SPECIES: LMB, SMB.

GERBUBBLE BUG

HOOK: Mustad 37189, sizes 1/0-4.

THREAD: Brown Monocord, 3/0.

TAIL: Four soft hen hackles, tied in pairs to flare.

HACKLE: Soft hen hackle wound over tail hackle butts.

WINGS: One soft hackle feather tied in at tail on each side, then pulled forward and tied off after most of body is completed. These side hackles should be buried in the deerhair so hackle fibers stick out at sides.

BODY: Deerhair spun and trimmed to shape.

NOTE: Adapted by Dave Whitlock from a 1920s hard-bodied pattern. Full directions are in his 1976 book *The Fly Tyer's Almanac.*

DIFFICULTY: 5.   SPECIES: LMB, SMB.

FLOATING FEATHER EEL

HOOK: Mustad 37189, sizes 1/0-4.

THREAD: Black Monocord, 3/0.

TAIL: Three to five long, thin saddle hackles, as in Feather Eel.

BODY: None.

HEAD/HACKLE: Deerhair to match tail in color, spun and trimmed to shape. Leave a few fibers at the rear of the head as a hackle collar. Plastic doll eyes glued on with five-minute epoxy.

NOTE: Colors as per sinking Feather Eel. Twitch slowly through the lily pads and hang on!

DIFFICULTY: 4.   SPECIES: LMB, SMB.

NOTES ON HOOKS:

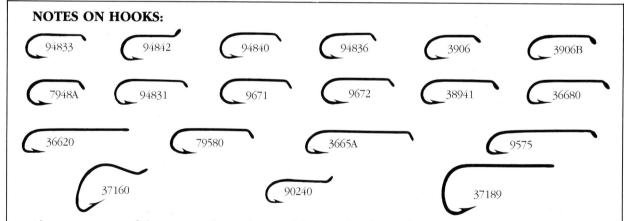

94833 94842 94840 94836 3906 3906B

7948A 94831 9671 9672 38941 36680

36620 79580 3665A 9575

37160 90240 37189

Above are some of the commonly used Mustad fly-tying hooks, each identified by model number for your reference. The 948 series hooks are generally used for dry flies, while the 3906 and 3906B are wet-fly hooks. They are followed by a series of nymph and streamer hooks. The 37160 hook is often used for caddis-larva patterns, while the 37189 "stinger" hook at far right is used for bass bugs where a large gap, or hook opening, is helpful. Other brands of hooks, such as Tiemco, Partridge, and VMC, are also commonly used, but Mustad has set the current standard by virtue of longevity and wide distribution.

FEATHER EEL

RABBIT-FUR LEECH

BUBBLE PUP

BLACK/WHITE HAIRBUG

GERBUBBLE BUG

FLOATING FEATHER EEL

(Flies shown 1.2 times actual size.)

THERE ARE UNFORTUNATELY thousands of fundamentalist fly tiers who march to fly specifications in lockstep, insisting on only the most literal following of established patterns as a means of fooling fish. Any fly pattern that has maintained its popularity over time—including most of the patterns in this book—is a formula for success, but that doesn't mean you can't alter the formula to suit your own needs.

As just one example, suppose you're tying nymphs for the Hendrickson hatch on your local trout stream. These insects—and all others—vary in color and, to a lesser extent, size from river to river and from region to region. Although a standard pattern for a Hendrickson nymph such as the one given in this book might work, it won't work as well as one you've specifically adapted in color and size to match the naturals in your particular river. All you need do is turn over some rocks in a riffle section of your river and look at some of the natural nymphs. Even more helpful is to examine the stomach contents of a freshly caught trout before its digestive juices have destroyed the insects upon which it has been feeding. In either case, you can quickly see if the nymphs are, for example, more olive than brown and a size 14 instead of a size 12. Then adapt your tying to suit.

Once you make the connection between your own fly tying and what's happening in the fish's world, your fly-tying and fishing success will increase immeasurably. You may, as many others have done, become deeply involved in studying aquatic entomology, the study of those insects that pass at least a portion of their life cycles in water. Such insects—mayflies, caddisflies, stoneflies, and so forth—are at various places and times important as fish food and thus important to you as a fly tier. (One of the best ways to start learning about aquatic entomology is by reading Ernest Schwiebert's 1955 book *Matching the Hatch*.) Trout, for example, have very sharp eyesight and sometimes exhibit incredible selectivity in feeding, especially if there's an abundance of one particular kind of insect. The brown trout in Vermont's Battenkill and the cutthroat trout of Wyoming's Yellowstone, for example, may both often view an off-color dry fly with the heartbreaking disdain of a New York art critic. For a fly tier, that's a large part of the challenge. If an established fly pattern won't work, improvise!

Like most things in fishing, the study of aquatic entomology has been carried to extremes by some, leading (especially among nonfishermen) to the caricature of a bespectacled fly fisherman waving a butterfly net and spouting Latin from the streamside bushes. Many people still fish success-fully with "little gray ones and big brown ones," dispensing with the scientific approach entirely. But the better your entomological understanding, the more fish you'll catch. You'll realize, for example, that many "old-fashioned" wet flies aren't so old-fashioned after all. The Little Marryat, for example, is a fine imitation of a hatching Sulphur Dun, and the shopworn Grizzly King does fairly well in imitating an egg-laying *Brachycentrus* caddisfly.

So far this discussion has been limited to trout, but the concept really applies to all fish sought with flies: find out what they're eating and tie a fly to match it. Striped bass, for example, are notoriously fussy about fly size. If the bass are eating five-inch-long sand eels in August, make your Simple Sand Eel fly five inches long. In October, when the sand eels are bigger, you'll want a fly that's about seven inches long. Bonefish are another example, and when you start bonefishing you'll quickly find that not all bonefish flies catch all the bonefish all the time. These fish can be very selective, and the wrong fly can send them off the flats like a panicked hurricane.

Atlantic salmon and steelhead are another puzzle. Although you may see either one seeming to rise or feed on rare occasions, for the most part they aren't eating during their upriver journeys. Well-established patterns are more important for these fish, as their response has been proven over time. That doesn't mean you shouldn't experiment, especially in the areas of fly color, size, and the action given a fly by different materials (soft versus stiff hackles, for example). Just be sure you've also made a good assortment of standard patterns to fall back on if your experiments don't prove out.

A few seasons ago in Vermont, we had an early, warm spring, and the Hendrickson mayfly hatch on the Battenkill, which usually happens in early May, took place in late April. The fishing was terrific. A friend called from New York in late April to announce his May 1 arrival to fish the hatch. When I told him the flies were gone, he insisted that was impossible, as the hatch timetable in his favorite fly-fishing book clearly stated the hatch would take place the first week in May. The lesson is obvious. While the fly patterns in this book have for the most part been enduring and successful, they are only a beginning. Don't let this or any other book create a gap between your thinking and your fishing.